Embrace Your Tomorrow... Today!

Discover how you can grasp the possibilities in your life.

by
Drs. R.L. and Ruby Yates and Family
Minister DeSean Yates
Minister Marcus & Naomi Yates
Minister Michael Yates
Minister Stephen Yates

"Build there an altar to the Lord your God, an altar of stones. Do not use any iron tool upon them. Build the altar of the Lord your God with fieldstones and offer burnt offerings on it to the Lord your God. Sacrifice fellowship offerings there, eating them and rejoicing in the presence of the Lord your God. And you shall write very clearly all the words of this law on these stones you have set up."

Deuteronomy 27: 5-8

Copyright © 2007 by Drs. R.L. and Ruby Yates and Family

Embrace Your Tomorrow... Today!
by Drs. R.L. and Ruby Yates and Family

Printed in the United States of America

ISBN 978-1-60266-218-6

All rights reserved solely by the author. The author guarantees all contents are original and do not infringe upon the legal rights of any other person or work. No part of this book may be reproduced in any form without the permission of the author. The views expressed in this book are not necessarily those of the publisher.

Unless otherwise indicated, Bible quotations are taken from the New International Version of the Bible. Copyright © 1995. By Zondervan Publishing House, Grand Rapids, MI 49530.

www.xulonpress.com

This book is dedicated to those who have poured into our lives:

In memory of our father and grandfather, the late
Deacon Robert Lee Yates, Sr.
who gave up this life for a crown...

September 20, 1920 – February 10, 1999

*He served our God, his family, and his fellow man.
A well lived life, A staunch example of sacrifice...
His footprints stand boldly in the sand!*

and to
our parents
Still in His Service
Mother Maggie Bumpers Yates
El Bethel Primitive Baptist Church
Mobile, Alabama
and
Rev. and Mrs. William A. Bunton, Jr.
Pastor and First Lady of the
Antioch Missionary Baptist Church
Buffalo, New York

You've invested so much in us that we must invest in others...

Preface

Embrace Your Tomorrow…TODAY!

In Mark chapter 10, the writer tells of a young man who seemed eager to embrace his future. We know him as The Rich Young Ruler. The reading of this passage gives us spiritual chills. Here is a man who has easily gained an audience with Jesus. He is unlike the woman with the issue of blood who had to press her way through the crowd, or Zacchaeus who had to climb a tree, or even Bartimaeus who could not see and had to depend upon the rumblings of those who said Jesus was passing by.

This young man had direct access to Jesus. God had him positioned so that he simply ran up to Jesus and knelt before Him. His path was unencumbered. He knew what he wanted. It is clear this young man saw acquiring possessions as the *sunom bonum* of his destiny. For him, eternal life was a possession to be added to his collection. He wanted to know what he could do to reach his destiny. It is not known how he came into riches or what life experiences his wealth had afforded him. We do know that riches had not brought him satisfaction because he was still searching. Somewhere he heard that Jesus had something he did not yet possess. No doubt he had stood by as Jesus blessed the children and wanted to be blessed himself.

As strange as it may seem, he allowed one thing to keep him from his destiny. Perhaps you too stand where he stood. There is but one thing that separates you from your destiny. For him, it was his possessions. Possessions represented his inability to empty himself out to God. He wanted to embrace, grab hold of his destiny, his tomorrow, but the wall that blocked his vision to the prize kept him from doing it that day. He was eager to tell Jesus what he had already done but unwilling to do one more thing. It is difficult to fathom how he could allow one thing to separate him from his destiny. Look at what he gave up to hold on to what would only pass away.

Are you ready to embrace all that God has for you? Make the decision to always put God first in your life. God has given you the gift of life. He has put a desire in you to do something with your life. Embrace your future today by allowing God to select who you partner with in life. Surround yourself with persons who want the same quality of life you want. Establish a love support system that is mutual and reciprocal. Connect with the right spiritual support system (people who desire spiritual growth). Join us as we look at words of strength and power that will help you embrace your tomorrow, today.

From Our Family to Yours
Be Blessed and Be a Blessing
Drs R.L. and Ruby Yates and Family
Minister DeSean, Minister Marcus and Naomi, Minister Michael and Minister Stephen

Heavenly Father, in the name of Your precious Son, Jesus the Christ, we release this work you have put into our hands. Amen

Table of Contents

		Page
Chapter 1	*What's Stopping You*..................................*11*	
	The Struggle To Believe 13	
	Who Am I?.. 15	
	Can God Really Use Me? 17	
	The Power of the Resurrection 19	
	Your Dream Child.................................... 21	
	This Is Your Time 23	
	When Jesus Was Amazed........................ 25	
Chapter 2	*Your Future Is Worth The Fight* *29*	
	Do The Possible. Expect The Impossible 31	
	Trusting God With Your Best 33	
	Why Me? 34	
	In The Midst of Bitterness 37	
	A Wise Woman Builds............................. 39	
	This Is The Time To Hope 43	
	Prepare For Your Inheritance.................. 44	
Chapter 3	*A Question of Control*	
	(Don't Lose Control of Your Garden).....*49*	
	Mis-Directed 51	
	There Is A Man In Every Boy.................. 53	
	The Flow From Your Life 55	
	The Value of the Mind 57	
	Healing For Mind, Body and Soul........................... 60	
	Think On These Things 62	
Chapter 4	*Cultivating A Revelation Testimony* *65*	
	Cultivating A Revelation Testimony........................ 65	
	From The Pasture To The Palace 67	
	Trusting God With Our Seed 69	
	Where There Is Unity…There Is Strength............... 70	

Table of Contents *(continued)*

Page

Remember Mama.. 72
Maturity 74
Build Your Life On Jesus.. 75

Chapter 5   *God Has Prepared You For Your Battle* 79
God Has Prepared You For Your Battle................... 79
How Can I Be Strong?... 81
There's Never Enough Time!.................................... 83
Follow The Leader... 84
Trusting God 101 85
What's A Father To Do?.. 87
It Took That... 89

Chapter 6   *Opportunity-You've Got It!*
Do You Want It? 99
Opportunity-You've Got It! Do You Want It? 99
Every Life Is Important 101
The Joy Of Salvation 102
The Joy of Salvation (Part 2) *Three Proofs of
Salvation* 103
A Welcome Shepherd.. 104
How Big Is God? 105
Get Up and Go Down Because God Is
Not Through With You 106

Chapter 7   *Deal or No Deal (Are You In or Out?)*................ 109
I Will Touch The World 112
A Mother's Love.. 111
Never Give Up... 114
Not Too Old For Vision 109
God Wants You!... 115
You've Been Sent 116

Chapter 1

What's Stopping You?

The greatest hindrance to embracing tomorrow is the tendency to hold on to yesterday. Paul had something to say to those who want everything God has for them. In Philippians he wrote about having a goal and totally committing to it. He suggests that we forget yesterday or those things behind and reach for the things in our future (Ephesians 1:13). What is it about yesterday that causes us to linger?

Lot's wife could not forget her yesterdays in Sodom and Gomorrah. As a result, she lost out on her future, stagnant outside the city gates; she refused to escape for her life (Genesis 19:26). So many others have held onto unforgiveness because their heart lingered in the past. There are those who hang on to the mistakes of the past and never give themselves a chance to live their future. Some live in the past because they fear what the future holds. This is the day for you to forget those things behind you and reach ahead to your future. Whatever your reason for hanging on to the past, follow the advice of the Apostle Paul and let it go.

Paul was in prison embracing a better future. He had left Troas where he had experienced a vision (Acts 16:9) of a man asking him to come to Macedonia to help them. When Paul arrived in Macedonia he found the unexpected. Sometimes the unexpected can drain us. We feel prepared to face certain battles and then the unexpected happens. They met a demon possessed girl. She was a slave girl who had been making money for her owners by telling fortunes. Paul commanded the spirit to come out of her in the name of Jesus. This brought about the unexpected. They were thrown in jail. Yet, even though he was locked up, he wrote a letter to the Christians to set their eyes on a higher goal and press toward it.

In pursuit of our tomorrows, it's important to consider what may be conscious or subconscious barriers to victory. Sometimes, we are our own greatest enemy. Let's consider the following principles as we attempt to prepare to clear the path to our destinies.

The Struggle To Believe

"The righteous shall live by faith." Habakkuk 2:4

Habakkuk is an interesting man. He is so earnest in his belief that he leaves himself open to be known by those who read this proclamation of faith. He is a man you want to get to know. This is a man who starts out with a question. Lord, how long will you ignore me? 'I'm struggling to trust you but when I look around, it looks as though you allow evil to go unpunished and faithful people like me have to struggle. Evil people seem to be winning the battle of life.

God tells Habakkuk His plan to use the Babylonians to punish the wicked. Habakkuk does not agree with the plan of God and accuses God of treating people like fish in the sea allowing the enemy to catch them with fish hooks and nets. Then he says, "I need an answer and I'm going to wait on God to answer me." Although he looked around and concluded that those around him had "the good life", his real struggle was the direction his life seemed to be taking.

Are you ever like Habakkuk? Having given God your best, do you struggle with the difficulties of life? Do you wonder why God doesn't do something about your situation? God's answer to Habakkuk was that faith has to be a way of life. God's message is that our trust in Him must not waver no matter what we see. We have to know that God is committed to us. In spite of our trials, God will bring us through them. He is committed to us.

Habakkuk thought he had too much drama in his life to write a vision. The prophet was struggling but he handled his struggle by spending time with God.

Life moves so fast, our list of things to do get so long that we sometimes leave out what is most needful. We must take our struggle with faith to God so that He can reassure us. It must not be ignored but reassured. Our faith is what holds us up. It is our support in the struggle of life. When life gets tough, our loving, faithful, Father God wants us to bring our faith struggle to Him.

Look at the gentle reassurance that God gives Habakkuk and find your reassurance there also. Habakkuk is discouraged and the faithful love of God encourages Him. The devil has cheated so many out of their encouragement from God because they feel ashamed because they struggle with their faith. Give that struggle to God. He is there for you. Be like Habakkuk (2:1). Stand like a guard and wait for God to strengthen your faith. You will be able to say like Habakkuk, "...the Lord answered me: Write down the revelation and make it plain." Habakkuk (2:2)

Who Am I?

"Who am I, that I should go to Pharaoh and bring the Israelites out of Egypt?" Exodus 3:11

The way God does things may seem unusual to us. If we were to pick a leader, we would not pick someone who had run out on his last battle. We would choose someone who was secure, confident in their abilities; sure they could do the job. But our God uses the insecure, the unsure, and the not so confident. It's amazing how God chooses those we consider unqualified and qualifies them.

Moses was the man of the hour called by God to lead a great exodus. But before he could lead this great mass of people out of Egypt, he had to experience his own exodus. Moses had to escape his own fears and insecurities.

As a baby, his life was in danger. After the king told the midwives to kill all the male babies that the Hebrew women gave birth to, Moses' mother saw that it was possible to save her son. She hid him for three months, then made a basket, coated it with tar and pitch, placed the child in the basket and floated him down the Nile. When found by the Pharaoh's daughter he was raised as a king's kid. Moses was initially very secure until one of his fellow Hebrews told him that he was no different than they were (Exodus 2:14). This shook Moses' world and he took flight. He was no longer secure; he was no longer certain about God's plan for his life. That sometimes happens in our lives. No one wants to admit they have insecurities because our understanding of it has a negative connotation. The good news is, God will take us as we are and shape us for His purpose. He will give us abilities and strengths that will make us able instruments in His hands.

God spoke to Moses and told him that He had heard the cry of His people. Moses thought he was the only one who saw the need or heard the cry. His attempt to solve the dilemma had been unsuccessful. Has God brought something to your attention that needs to be resolved? You've heard the cry, seen the need? Ask Him if He wants to use you in the resolution.

There is so much pain in our world. So many people are hurting, just needing someone to respond to their cry for help. We tend to see ourselves as unable to help because we have our own dilemmas. Moses was a fugitive, taken in by strangers, but God helped him look beyond his situation and see the needs of others. What about you? Today is your opportunity.

Can God Really Use Me?

"And also some women who had been cured of evil spirits and diseases: Mary, called Magdalene from whom seven demons had come out." St. Luke 8:2

In the gospel according to Luke, we are given a very personal story about Mary Magdalene. Mary was a vulnerable woman. No doubt she was unpopular and disrespected by the community in which she lived. Luke says that Jesus had cast seven demons out of her. What torment she must have known! It is no wonder that the tomb was not the only thing empty that first Easter morning. Mary's heart felt as empty as the tomb. The person who had made a difference in her life had been brutally murdered and now His body was gone.

There is no doubt about her love for Jesus. She was present at His crucifixion, present at his burial, and she was there bright and early on resurrection morning. According to John, she was actually the very first person to see the resurrected Christ. But most of all, Mary had learned so much from Jesus. His relationship with her was not just Savior but He was her Master and Teacher. We know this because her first word to our resurrected Lord was Rabboni. "Mary!" Jesus said (John 20:16). She turned toward Him and cried in Aramaic, 'Rabboni!' (which means Teacher), or you who has authority over me). Just as He had authority over Mary, Christ has full authority over every person who has submitted themselves to Him.

There is much wisdom to be gained from Mary's commitment to Christ. When she noticed that someone had rolled the stone away she sought help because she thought His body was stolen. While others saw the empty tomb and went back to their daily routine, Mary remained at the tomb. She did not give up easily. This Jesus, the Christ, had healed her brokenness and allowed her to unveil her torment.

Because we are aware of our vulnerability, it seems so hard sometimes to yield completely to Jesus. We somehow want to leave some guard or protection that we can fall back on just in case. This was not the case with Mary Magdalene. She opened her life up to Christ and as a result experienced deliverance. With Christ we can reveal all because He loves us as we are. No wonder she hurried to share the good news. She had to tell the salvation story because she had experienced it. Mary Magdalene was a wise woman who planted the salvation story in the hearts of others.

"The Power of the Resurrection"

"Then Jesus came to them and said, 'All authority in heaven and on earth has been given to me.' " Matthew 28:18

Did you know that there is a level of power that comes forth directly as a result of the resurrection of Jesus Christ? Understanding power helps the struggle we sometimes have facing our challenges with confidence.

There are two words in the Greek that teach us the New Testament meaning of power. One is found in John 1:12 and the other in Romans 1:16. The writer, John, teaches about the position we receive when we become a son or daughter of God and Romans speaks about the kind of power that overcomes resistance. It is important to understand that Jesus gave us both through His resurrection.

The resurrection has power because the crucifixion was real. In it, Jesus had spiritual pain; Jesus had emotional pain, and Jesus had physical pain. Because of His position in God as His only begotten Son, He overcame death and was resurrected or brought back to life.

Humans see death as a power greater than our knowledge and ability. We do not have the power to put life into a dead body ourselves, so it baffles us. We know that Jesus was completely dead yet God used His ability to raise Him from the dead. This does so much for our faith. We have courage in our everyday lives because we know that the God who raised Jesus from the dead also has our back (Psalm 62:7). We have courage for the future because we know that the God who raised Jesus will also one day raise us up to live with Him eternally. The power of the resurrection is not just Jesus being raised from the dead (Matthew 28: 6), it is also knowing that Jesus has the power and will raise you from your situations that seem impossible. But in order for Jesus to raise you from your situation, you have to die to the hold that it has on you.

As I sign off, I want you to know that no matter what you have done or where you have been, Jesus will forgive you and He will save you and raise you out of your situation. So if you want to be forgiven and saved and resurrected out of the situation that you are in, then I want you to pray this prayer with me. Dear Lord, I know that I have sinned and right now Lord, I repent of my sin. At this moment I receive you as my Lord and Savior. Amen. God is powerful, man!

Your Dream Child

"Where is your wife Sarah?" they asked him. "There, in the tent," he said. Then the Lord said, "I will surely return to you about this time next year, and Sarah your wife will have a son." Now Sarah was listening at the entrance to the tent, which was behind him. Abraham and Sarah were already old and well advanced in years, and Sarah was past the age of childbearing. So Sarah laughed to herself as she thought, "After I am worn out and my master is old, will I now have this pleasure?" Then the Lord said to Abraham, "Why did Sarah laugh and say, 'Will I really have a child, now that I am old?' Is anything too hard for the Lord?"
Genesis 18:9-14

Now Sarah was listening to this conversation from the tent nearby. And since Abraham and Sarah were both very old, and Sarah was long past the age of having children, she laughed silently to herself...Why did Sarah laugh? Why did she say, 'Can an old woman like me have a baby? Is anything too hard for the LORD?"

Read this word again! Isn't this just like us as women of God? Sarah wasn't even supposed to be listening. She was in a different tent. Are we laughing at the possibilities of God? We have to ask ourselves why Sarah laughed and why we are laughing. Sarah laughed because she looked within. Looking within she could not see the ability of God but only her inability. It was the dream of every woman in Israel to bare a son for her husband.

Your dream child may be a new start in life, financial, physical or mental deliverance. In Sarah's case, she was barren and unable to produce a son for Abraham. She had come to accept it and went on with life. Even though she gave up, we know that Sarah experienced the blessing of God and thus her dream child.

What can we learn from this experience? Our dreams and aspirations seem from difficult to impossible when we look to ourselves for our miracles. There are just three things I would like for you to consider in order to gain the strength you need for your dream child.

First of all, you need the courage to look away from yourself. By that I mean, don't be your own limitation. Your blessing is not limited to what you can provide. You can do all things through Christ who strengthens you (Philippians 4:13).

The second thing I want you to consider is sanctification or setting yourself apart from everyone and everything for a period of time each day. Start with one half hour. With this time, read the word of God and pray. My suggestion is that you start with the book of Ruth. There is so much in the book of Ruth that helps us to make a decision to change direction and go with God's flow.

Finally, surrender. Yield your will to the will of God. Look beyond your impossibilities to His possibilities. Once we clearly hear God's will for us, Satan tries to get us to defy it. We think there must be an easier or better way than God's way. Resist the devil. Do it God's way. Things will begin to happen. God will move on your behalf.

Sarah found herself in a situation where disbelief was her response to what seemed an impossibility. Keep your eyes on the possibilities of God. Know that He can do what you cannot do. He can see where you cannot see. He can move things that are immovable to you. Put your hope on target. Put it into possibility by turning to God.

This Is Your Time

"Who knows but that you have come to royal position for such a time as this." Esther 4:14

A short time ago, we celebrated the home going of a great woman of faith and courage in the person of Dr. Coretta Scott King. We honor her as we walk into our own destiny to follow her example in allowing God to use us wherever He places us.

Many times we look at the adversity in our lives and the seemingly smooth sailing of others and wonder when our mountain will level or will life continue to be an up hill climb? We wonder when our road will be smooth, or when the sun will peek through the clouds in our lives. Then we read the book of Esther, or see the life of a Coretta Scott King, and remember that God chose us for such a time as this.

At a time in Israel's history when they faced annihilation, God set the stage for deliverance. Who knew that God would allow King Xerxes who ruled over 127 provinces from India to Ethiopia, to marry this young Jewish girl so that she would be in place to save her people? The wicked Prime Minister, Haman, had been planted in position by Satan to wipe out the people of God, but through Esther, God saved His people. The people of God fasted and Esther became the intercessor before the king. It's wonderful to see how God used Esther who said, "Go and gather together all the Jews of Shushan fast for me... I will go to the king and if I perish, I perish." (Esther 4:16) It's exciting to look at the life of Esther and her God given opportunity. It's wonderful to see how God used Mrs. King. It is said that she once said that she married more than a man, that she married a vision and a destiny.

But God also has a dramatic story for your life. He has placed you where you are in order to prepare you for His use. At just the right time, God directs history to use you for His glory. This is your time to fulfill your destiny, to do all that God has given you to do. Nothing can stop you if you walk in faith. The task ahead of you is never as great as the power within you; for God has said that, "The one who is in you is greater than the one who is in the world."

(1 John 4:4) "We can do all things through Christ who strengthens us." (Philippians 4:13) "We are more than conquerors through Christ who loved us" (Romans 8:37). Your place of destiny may not be at the king's palace as with Esther, but this is your time to fulfill your purpose. This is your time to have the commitment to do what God has given you to do and to give the response that Esther gave, "And Even though it is against the law, I will go to see the king. If I must perish, I perish." I am willing to. (Esther 4:16) What are you willing to sacrifice for God's purpose?

When Jesus Was Amazed

"When Jesus heard this, he was amazed at him and turning to the crowd following him, he said, I tell you, I have not found such great faith even in Israel." Luke 7:9

Luke shares an experience where Jesus and His disciples were in Capernaum when a centurion, a Roman army officer, approached them with a need. This man had other men under his command and knew the power of authority. He knew that when he spoke, those under his authority had to respond. The centurion had a servant who was sick to the point of death and wanted Jesus to heal him.

Jesus looked beyond his need and saw his faith. Jesus looked at his faith and said, "I have not found such great faith even in Israel." Of course, because Jesus was eternal, He had seen the faith of Abraham who hoped against hope that his dead body would bring forth life (Romans 4:18). He had seen the faith of David that stood against a Philistine giant. He had the ability to even look beyond the years of this man (1Samuel 17:32) and see the faith of Smith Wigglesworth, Kathryn Kuhlman, and Oral Roberts.

Our faith is visible to God even when it is not visible to others. He looks beyond what others see and knows that we are depending on Him with all the hope that is within us. Just as He responded to the centurion, He responds to us. I have decided to totally lean on Jesus. I know His love for me. I have experienced His compassion. I've lived to see so many deliverances. Time after time I've witnessed His faithfulness. He has blessed me and stood by me. Let me be your witness. Receive my testimony and know that you can depend on God. Look beyond your situation and experience the power and faithfulness of God. When life is tough trust Him to move in your situation. Let Jesus look at your back against the wall and see your faith shine beyond your situation. Has anything ever caused you to just look at it and marvel, to be impressed to the point that you could only say "Awesome." The song writer said that our God is an awesome God. Jesus says, my servant has awesome faith.

Questions for Discussion

Chapter 1

Section One
The Struggle To Believe

1. Can you identify with the sentiments of Habakkuk?
2. Have you ever found it difficult to truly trust God when everywhere you look it seems that those who aren't living for God are winning in life while those who commit themselves to Him suffer?
3. Do you wonder why God doesn't do something about your situation?
4. Have you tried to take your questions to God?

Section Two
Who Am I?

1. What qualities do you look for in a leader?
2. What qualities do you see in yourself that would cause God to select you?
3. Have you ever gone from security to insecurity?
4. Choose a person who knows you pretty well. Ask them to name some of your characteristics that they see as strengths. Did they name strengths you were not aware of?

Section Three
Can God Really Use Me?

1. What things leave you vulnerable?
2. How do you deal with emptiness?

Section Four
The Power Of The Resurrection

1. How do we have power as a result of our position?
2. What things have gripped you and lost their hold?
3. How did you participate in the process of God moving you to victory?

Section Five
Your Dream Child

1. What is your dream?
2. Does it seem possible?
3. What steps have you taken to bring it to pass?

Section Six
This Is Your Time

1. Look around you. Where has God placed you?
2. Identify a challenge you have faced.
3. How did you resolve it?

Section Seven
When Jesus Was Amazed

1. Does the struggle to believe seem winnable?
2. Do you think Christ is surprised by your faith?

Chapter 2

Your Future Is Worth The Fight!

Genesis 28:8-22

God's message to you today is to hold on to the promise. You stand in a situation that you don't understand but God has positioned you. You are in a place of blessing. Don't focus on what it looks like to the physical eye but focus on the promise of God. He has taken you to the place of blessing. When Israel was in Egypt they were slaves in a foreign land but God told them that this was a place of blessing. The place of struggle, the place of bondage can also be the place where God decides to bless you. God told them that every person should borrow from his neighbor when moved from bondage to deliverance. After leaving Egypt, they went to the wilderness rather than directly into their promised blessing. But God said the wilderness, the dry and desolate place where there was no food or water, would be a place of blessing for them.

We need to understand that the place of blessing is the place where God deems it so. It doesn't matter if there is bondage in the physical place or if it is a barren wilderness. It doesn't matter if the physical place has nobody working, wayward children, lost spouse, or the enemy has risen up against you. God said the place you are in is a place of blessing.

In our scripture lesson today, both Esau and Jacob had a blessing pronounced on them. The difference was that Esau chose disobedience while Jacob chose to obey and embrace the promise. Now when I tell you to embrace the promise, embrace sounds like a soft word, but to the contrary, it is power-packed! In order to embrace the promise, you have to invest all that you have in the promise, every bit of strength, every bit of faith, every bit of finance, every bit of all that you have. You've got to decide if you want to get your provision from God's hand or from your hand.

Jacob opened himself to vision, that is, he was willing to see what God wanted to show him. He made a connection with God by means of a stairway or ladder. This took him from where he was to where God was. There was a struggle on that ladder but it was worth the fight. Jacob's future was dependent on it. Then Jacob began to worship. Jacob made a commitment. Jacob entered into covenant with God. His place of blessing became a place of meeting God, a place of vision, a place of connection, a place of worship, a place of commitment, a place of covenant and a place of blessing. God said, "Jacob, I am the Lord." (vs. 13) Now, to tell Jacob that he was Lord meant that God was his ruler and the ruler of a household is responsible to those under him.

God was presenting Himself as Jacob's provider. So God said, "I am the Lord. I will give you and your descendants the land you are lying on. There will be as many people in your family as there is dust on the ground. Then I will spread you out from the east to the west. I will spread you out from the north to the south. I will enlarge your territory. Everybody else on the earth will be blessed but that blessing will come through you. Jacob, I will be with you and watch over you and bring you back to this land. Jacob said this must be, this has to be the house of God. Here I have heard the plan of God, I have received the anointing of God and I will run to my destiny (vs. 13-15).

Do The Possible. Expect The Impossible!

"She came up behind him and touched the edge of his cloak."
Luke 8:44

Luke teaches about the power of Jesus by giving us episodes in the lives of people. They could almost be headlines in the newspaper, "A Woman Kisses Jesus' Feet", "Jesus Calms A Storm", "Jesus Sets A Demon Possessed Man Free". No doubt Luke's mind was completely blown.

Then he tells us about a woman who touched Jesus and was healed of a disease that no doctor had been able to cure. For twelve years she had suffered. She had been held captive by a hemorrhaging condition and could find no cure. No doubt, she was physically, emotionally, spiritually and financially drained. Luke shows that no matter how desperate your situation may be, Jesus can turn despair into hope. By faith, the power of God did the impossible. Doctors had looked at her situation and said, "IMPOSSIBLE!". The bank had looked at her finances and said, "IMPOSSIBLE!". Yet, something on the inside of this woman kept pushing and hoping and believing. She did the possible but expected the impossible.

Our situations are too desperate to stand alone. We have got to touch Jesus with our faith for deliverance. The faith of this woman touched Jesus before her hand ever reached out to touch Him. She didn't know everything there was to know about the power of God. She thought she could secretly touch Him. God knows every pain we feel, every tear that falls from our eyes, every groan of our voice and He cares. I can just feel the weariness of this woman. She feels alone. She feels as though no one understands what she is going through. Trembling, she told Jesus what she was going through. She fell to her knees and told Him why she had touched Him.

Luke told the story well, but only a person who has suffered then touched Jesus with their faith can really know how she must have felt. Jesus responded. He healed her and He owned her. He said, "...daughter, your faith has healed you, Go in peace." (Luke 8:48) You too can say, "Jesus; I reach out to you and touch you with my faith. I am your daughter (or I am your son). Deliver me from this issue that has held me captive." There is a cure for what holds you captive. Just reach out in faith... touch Jesus.

Trusting God With Your Best

"I am gathering a few sticks to take home and make a meal for myself and my son that we may eat—and die." 1 Kings 17:12 (NIV)

A wise person gives out of their need. They do not wait until there is an abundance because giving out of our need means that we give out of our faith. We give before we have that extra strength knowing that God will give strength where there is weakness, provision in our lack. We give to others when we have a need ourselves, and over and over we receive the blessing of God.

We wonder why our parents and grandparents seemed to have had so little, yet they shared so much. It is because in giving out of their need, God multiplied their resources. There were eight of us including my parents and my cousin. Every Sunday each of us brought several friends home from church. We saw our mother take a chicken with 7 parts and feed 18 people and we were all filled. My mother cooked out of her faith.

There is another woman who gave out of her need. We have come to know her as the widow of Zarephath (1Kings 17:8-24). God sent Elijah to this widow and we wonder, no doubt he was wondering… 'Didn't God know that she was preparing to eat her last meal and die?' Yet He sent the man of God to say, 'don't be afraid but cook what you have out of your faith and put God first.' So this woman partnered with God and her last became a seed for a great harvest. A wise person turns the last they have into a seed. The woman at Zarephath planted that one seed and it became the first of a great crop. She now had enough in her meal barrow to continue to eat.

Having the courage to use our last allows us to glorify God. It allows us to use our faith. It invites God into our situation to build a foundation of plenty, of provision, of power. We learn that when we allow God to touch what we have, there is always an abundance. A wise person puts their lack, whether it is spiritual, physical or financial, into the hands of God. My deepest need and my greatest concerns are in His hands for His touch.

Why Me?

Romans 8:16-18; Luke 8:43-48

Why me? Why do I suffer? Why do I have pain? Why do people who don't seem to deserve it prosper while I struggle? Why do I keep failing over and over again? Have you ever found yourself asking these questions? "Why me?" is a downward spiral that plagues countless people day in and day out. It is the roadblock that they cannot cross, the anchor that stagnates them midstream, and the sorrowful song by which they cry themselves to sleep at night.

This battle is not just fought in the lives of unbelievers, but it's surprisingly even more evident amongst believers. We, as believers, are oftentimes guilty of viewing our faith in an oversimplified and distorted version of Christianity that we market to one another. This view says that if we do right, nothing bad will happen. Then when something bad happens, we assume that we were either doing something wrong and God was punishing us, or that we were living right and the devil was attacking us.

While some suffering is genuinely self-inflicted, and some suffering is due to demonic attack, I believe that there is suffering that originated from the simple fact that life is hard. As Christians, we seem to have a difficult time accepting that. Thus, we find it even more difficult to reconcile the fact that God would allow us to suffer without having anyone to blame. We waste untold amounts of energy attempting to find out whose fault our struggle is, and we miss the fact that God is using our suffering, regardless of its source, to promote us.

Sometimes suffering is the method that God uses to get us where we're going. Just as Jesus had to experience Gethsemane, the place of crushing, before He could be elevated to his position of glory on the cross, we must go through seasons of suffering to put us in our place in God. This is the essence of Paul's reflections in Romans 8:16-18. Paul said we must share in Christ's suffering if we expect to share in His glory. We must be able to handle suffering in order to handle glory. So how do we handle our issues in light of this?

What's Your Issue?

This woman's story is one of the most amazing examples of the power of God to overcome suffering. This nameless woman, referred to only as the woman with the "issue", had been facing her battle for many years. In fact, she had become so accustomed to her situation that it had sunk down to the core of her person. It was a part of her paradigm. It governed how she viewed the world. This woman's ailment was more than a condition, but it had become her identity. Physically, her "issue" was similar to a hemorrhage, a constant outflow of blood that rendered her weak and prone to sickness and disease. Can you imagine? This woman struggled for twelve years with a wound that could not be seen on the surface, but that bled uncontrollably on the inside and wouldn't heal. No one else could see the extent of her damage. Only she knew how badly she was wounded, but, in spite of her almost frantic attempts to stop the hurting, she couldn't make her issue go away. And, because there seemed to be no answer, she resigned to live with the question, "Why me?"

This is the struggle of countless individuals who faithfully put masks on every Sunday and fill the pews of America's churches. We love God and we believe his promises, but many of us have battled the pain of suffering for so long that we've allowed it to define us. We've accepted our issues as the cross we were meant to bear and have, thus, yielded to the sentence of perpetual bleeding.

Though some of us have a hard time reconciling why she, a believer, would be allowed by God to go through this for twelve years, there was a purpose. If she had not gone through the suffering, she would never have received a deeper revelation of Jesus as her healer that day. Suffering leads to revelation. Paul says in verse 18, "I consider that our present sufferings are not worth comparing with the glory (doxa) that will be revealed in us". The deeper your revelation of God is, the more glory that is generated. Paul is saying, "When I add up every bruise that I receive from suffering and compare it to the revelation I receive of Jesus Christ through my suffering, it is not even worthy of comparing." You might have been sick, but now you know Him as Healer. You might have been struggling to make ends meet, but now you know Him as a provider.

I want to share three principles of seasonal sufferings with you.

Principles of Seasonal Suffering

Principle #1: Losers quit, but winners fight.

This woman decided she was going to get in the presence of God. This was no easy task as she had many barriers. Her body said that she wasn't strong enough. She had physical discomfort. Her mind said that she wasn't worthy. She had shame and insecurity. The fact is, you will always have a reason to stay in your season, but how many know that if you're willing to fight, you can win?

Principle #2: It's worth the reach.

When she got to Jesus, she had to decide whether or not she was going to reach out to Him. In doing so, she was taking the risk that she might reach out and nothing would happen. People that have been through trauma are sometimes hesitant about reaching because they don't think that they can bear the disappointment of being let down again. She did not let this stop her. She didn't have any more options. She realized that He was her only hope.

Desperation will give you the momentum to reach out to Jesus, no matter what the cost.

Principle #3: Recognize your son-ship.

When Jesus announced her deliverance, He called her "daughter". It was always in His plan to deliver her, but He had to make sure she would know who to give the praise to when it happened. Paul said in verses 16 and 17, "you are children," but, your son-ship connects you to two equally important parts of your inheritance, suffering and glory.

Suffering has a purpose: to prepare you for your next level of blessing. Hold your head up. Tell all the haters, "I'm in transition, "I'm suffering my way to glory," It may not always feel like it, but you are the son of a King and you're being transitioned into glory. This confession was important for the woman to embrace.

In The Midst Of Bitterness

Ruth 1

As I was awakened from sleep by the voice of the Lord, He was whispering something in my ear about love. He told me that the kind of love Ruth had for Naomi was a love expressed in the midst of bitterness. I began to think about it and remembered when Naomi had returned to Bethlehem from Moab she told the people to call her Mara because she felt the Lord had dealt with her bitterly. At the point when Ruth had uttered those renowned words, "Urge me not to leave thee…. (Ruth 1:16) she made her inheritance confession. This is what I call Ruth's 'don't ask me to leave you commitment.' Naomi was a bitter woman. Still Ruth entered into covenant. Ruth partnered into the Abrahamic covenant. She followed God to a land she did not know. She underwent the circumcision because the idolic Moabite religion was cut away. Thereby cutting herself away from the idols of Moab she said, 'your God shall be my God'. God made Ruth's name great. He blessed her, blessed those who blessed her, cursed those who cursed her. He made her a blessing to others. She entered covenant with God when she made her, "Don't ask me to leave you statement.'

This was not a statement Ruth made back in the good old days before death took it's toll on the family, but she made it in the midst of Naomi's bitterness. Naomi was bitter because she had lost what was most important to her, her husband and her children. In the midst of this, Ruth makes her 'Don't ask me to leave you' commitment. Her oath was before God and Naomi. 'If anything but death shall part us, may God deal with me' (Ruth 1:17). Imagine making the journey from Moab to Bethlehem with a bitter mother-in-law. Ruth had the God kind of love that saved us while we were still sinners. (Romans 5:8) She loved Naomi in the midst of her bitterness. She had the God kind of love that forgives over and over again.

You too can love in the midst of your situation. You too can forgive again and await the change of God in the heart of your loved one. Read the story. It was after Naomi arrived in Bethlehem that she announced that she was still bitter. The ministry of love had no reward for Ruth as of yet, but Ruth continued her ministry of love. She went to the fields of Boaz and gleaned that they might have food. She lived day in and day out and took counsel from a bitter woman without reward from her.

Finally, Boaz said, "May the Lord repay you for what you have done. May you be richly rewarded by the Lord, the God of Israel under whose wings you have come to take refuge." (Ruth 2:12) The reward for her love ministry in the midst of bitterness did not stop there. Ruth became the wife of Boaz. She and Boaz had a son named Obed who had a son named Jesse who had a son named David and out of the lineage of David came our Lord and Savior, Jesus Christ. Make the commitment. God will reward you.

A Wise Woman Builds

"The wise woman builds her house, but with her own hands the foolish one tears hers down." Proverbs 14:1
Read Matthew 15:21; Mark 7:24-30

At a very young age, my children told whoever would listen that the wisest woman they knew was my mother. As I think of the many teaching moments I spent with her, I am inclined to agree. She certainly was a builder in my life. This has helped me to strive to be a wise woman making every effort to pour into the lives of others just as my life has been poured into. Life building is a commitment to pour into the life of another person without regard to the sacrifice required.

God has placed us where we are, equipped to build, to fill the lives of others in a way that fixes what is broken from the inside out. The writer of Proverbs helps us to understand the choice we have of building or foolishly plucking down. We live in a broken world, filled with broken communities and broken lives. Sometimes we must pour into those lives at the expense of our sacrifice.

Sometimes the brokenness we have been assigned to is in our world, or community. Just as with this Syro-Phoenician woman, sometimes the brokenness is in our own home. Jesus had just poured out of Himself teaching a lesson that was difficult for the scribes and Pharisees. It was a lesson on tradition and ceremony in the church. It was a lesson to a people who were steeped in tradition. I can imagine it was so draining that Jesus secluded himself to be refreshed. He left and went to a house in Tyre and Sidon.

Although this was not publicized, a woman whose daughter had an unclean spirit heard that He was there and cried out for help. This woman wanted to build her house, but she had a devil in the house. She needed Jesus to empty the house by casting the devil out so that it could be rebuilt.

Sometimes our approach is to try to fix things ourselves, but this woman went to Jesus. It was not convenient because no one was even supposed to know where Jesus was, but she sought Him and found Him. Scripture says He could not be hid.

The determination to build her house was greater than anything that could hinder her. Building our homes must be a priority. This woman wasn't just starting a new home. It was a home that was already established, but already in trouble. It had to be torn down before it could be built up. The devil had her home in a mess. The devil had to be cast out before a new foundation could be laid. She had the blessing of two in one. The same man could tear down the old and build up the new. Jesus could do both demolition and foundation work. Jesus could tear down the old by casting out the devil and He could lay Himself as a new foundation. She had the right man for the job. It took determination. She was not willing to give up. She had to interrupt Jesus from his rest. He had gone into seclusion possibly for re-energizing and re-filling.

This woman had no promise. She was not a Jew. Jesus had come to the lost house of Israel. He had come to rebuild Israel so that they could become builders. She had to ask for a blessing that was not rightfully hers. She did not deserve it but the grace of God was available. When Jesus told her to get in line, that He had to minister to Israel first, she was not too proud to plead with Him. She was already at the feet of Jesus and refused to get up without a blessing. Jesus responded and cast the devil out of her daughter without ever being in the presence of the daughter.

Visualize it in your mind. As the woman approached the house, she could no doubt feel that the presence of God had been in her home. She walked in the door and saw a delivered daughter lying on the bed. So it is with your house. The deliverance of God is available for you and your entire household. Of all the prestigious and lofty things that are built in life, the greatest builders are those who build lives.

How do we build our homes and what actions constitute tearing the home down? Every home must have a good foundation. Pray as this woman did for your home. Homes are built by atmosphere. What we say creates atmosphere. Although words create climate in a home, it's not always what you say but how you say it. Look at our words as salt. The word of God says in Colossians 4:6 "Let your conversation be always full of grace, seasoned with salt so that you may know how to answer everyone." We have to remember that salt seasons as it preserves but in an open wound it also burns. The words we speak can build or destroy. We must be especially careful with the young as they try generational fads as they find their identity. Be careful not to destroy their hearts. A Christian delivery man made a delivery to our church. He was introduced to two of our young ministers who were introduced to him as such. He told one of them that he looked like a preacher because of the way he dressed. He told the other he didn't believe he was a preacher because he wore his cap backwards. You could see the countenance of the young man drop. He had stood proudly as he was introduced. He loved to preach the word of God. I spoke to the person who was delivering. I told him he seemed to be a very sincere Christian. I asked him what scripture he got that from. He was adamant that young people in the "world" wore their caps backward and if this young man wanted to preach, he should turn his cap around to be separated from the "world". I asked him if he knew how the established church felt about Jesus. They criticized Him and refused to receive Him. After much discussion, I told him to be careful that he didn't one day stand before God's judgment to answer for turning young people away from God because he judged them.

We must remember that God calls us to be fishers of men. Catch souls. Feed them the word. Don't try to clean them before you catch them. Things like dress and music are sometimes the identity of a generation not conditions for salvation or call to ministry.

As we touch lives in the building process, we must guard our tongues. Even in discipline, the selection and tone of our words can either build or tear down a life. Make the commitment to preserve your family members, to build others and encourage them. God made us to support one another, to help each other through the tough times.

This is the Time to Hope

"The men who were guarding Jesus began mocking and beating Him. They blindfolded Him and demanded, 'Prophesy! Who hit you?' And they said many other insulting things to Him.
St Luke 22: 63-65

The disciples had gained so much confidence as they walked with Christ daily. They had watched as He gave sight to the blind, cast out demons, healed the dreaded disease of leprosy, and even spoke life into the dead. But now a tragic thing had happened. Their eyes had witnessed the blessed Lord fall into the hands of the chief priest and elders, stand trial and be condemned to die. Too frightened to do anything but go into hiding, they stood by as He was taken from judgment hall to judgment hall, beaten until His flesh ripped open.

All they could remember was the horror of the moment. They could not remember that He said men would tear His body (temple) down but God would raise it in three days. They had promised to follow Him even to death, but fear sat in and they yielded to the weakness of the flesh. How disappointing and hopeless life seemed to them now. The gloom that loomed over the Christian world was unimaginable. Everything they had hoped for and fought for now seemed so impossible. The enemy had ripped away the disciples hope with their evil deeds. Little did they know that this was the time to hope.

I know that you can identify with those disciples who were so close to Christ, because you too deal with your share of disappointment. You too have experienced those times when the darkness of the past loomed over you like a heavy cloud and the turbulence of your yesterday defined your tomorrow. But God had a remedy for the pain and disappointment felt by those early disciples and He has a remedy for your pain and disappointment too.

Of course you live in difficult days, but these are days that God can and will see you through. If you have had the foundation of your hope ripped from beneath you, there are three suggestions I have for you. (1) Don't let your future be defined by your past. (2) Face your misplaced expectation. (3) Allow God to give you a new direction.

No matter what you go through, you can decide not to let your past determine your future. So many people hold on to the hurt and pain of the past, never asking God for strength and direction for the future. Secondly, you must face your misplaced expectation. Even though Jesus told the disciples what was going to happen, they continued to have their own expectations. The disciples wanted immediate victory without the bumps in the road. You cannot allow trials and unexpected challenge to hold you hostage. For sure, no one looks for hard times, but when they come, don't be thrown off guard to the point that you give up. Finally, when things don't go as you expected, ask God for renewed strength and dedication to the vision and direction He gives.

There is hope! There is a reason to look up and expect God to move in your life. You can trust God to do what's best for you. Romans 8:28 says, "And we know that in all things God works for the good of those who love him, who have been called according to his purpose." This is the time to hope.

Prepare For Your Inheritance

"Then Joshua son of Nun secretly sent two spies from Shittim. "Go, look over the land," he said, "especially Jericho." So they went and entered the house of a prostitute named Rahab and stayed there. The king of Jericho was told, "Look! Some of the Israelites have come here tonight to spy out the land." So the king of Jericho sent this message to Rahab: "Bring out the men who came to you and entered your house, because they have come to spy out the whole land." But the woman had taken the two men and hidden them. Joshua 2:1-4

Rahab was a woman who did not grow up in Bible class. She was not the lead singer in the church choir. In fact, she lived a life that was not praise worthy at all. Rahab was a Canaanite who served idol gods. She was a woman who was caught between her destiny and her circumstances, between her yesterday and her tomorrow. God gave her intuition that caused her to make a decision that led her into a great inheritance. Given the choice to stand with the people of God and gain a new inheritance or take the way of a people filled with fear, she made the right choice. Rahab took the way of faith.

What she had was a given. Her style of life was certain and had allowed her to become a prosperous business woman. She had heard about Israel's God and His faithfulness but had no personal experience with Him. She had no testimony that God had heard her prayers, no proof that He would make a way out of no way for her. Would this God of Israel give her an inheritance? Should she look beyond the failures of her past and hope for a better future?

Often our readiness to receive something better requires that we have the faith to step away from what seems sure. Rahab rehearsed what she had heard about God and made a step of trust. She could have helped the Jewish spies yet not looked for salvation for herself or her family. She could have worried about what others said and taken the scarlet cord from her window. It was decision time and she made the decision to have something better. Opportunity was knocking at her door and she was going to take that opportunity.

I have a son who says, "Mom, if I succeed I'm in God's hands and if I fail I'm still in God's hands. I'd rather fail than never try." This is a good philosophy. Your desire to receive your inheritance has to be greater than your fear of failure.

What have you heard about the faithfulness of God? Perhaps you have more than Rahab had, you have personal experience of the faithfulness of God. You know without a doubt that He will never leave you nor forsake you. Or maybe you are like Rahab and have only heard about the faithfulness of God. Try Him. He will not fail you. Don't let anything stop you from receiving all that God has for you. Now is the time to decide to go after what you want in life. It's your inheritance, your gift from God. It belongs to you! Get ready. Prepare to receive your inheritance!

Questions for Discussion

Chapter Two
Your Future Is Worth The Fight

Section One
Do The Possible. Expect The Impossible!

1. What was this woman's vision?
2. What were the possibilities?
3. What were the impossibilities?
4. Examine your vision. Separate the possibilities and impossibilities. Do they change as you get closer to the manifestation of the vision?

Section Two
Trusting God With Your Best

1. What was the woman's faith like before she gave?
2. Why was the cake the woman's best?
3. What is your best?

Section Three
Why Me?

1. How does God use suffering?
2. Do bad things happen to good people?
3. What does Romans 8:28 mean in light of this section?
4. What is seasonal suffering?

Section Four
In The Midst Of Bitterness

1. What does the "Don't ask me to leave you" commitment mean to you?
2. What are the benefits of endurance?

Section Five
A Wise Woman Builds

1. Is building your home a priority?
2. How can you apply the usage of salt in the atmosphere of your home?

Section Six
This Is The Time To Hope

1. Why do you think a daily walk with Christ can increase your confidence?
2. If you are suffering from a relapse in hope, what can you do?

Section Seven
Prepare For Your Inheritance

1. What was Rahab's response to what she had heard about the people of God?
2. What characteristics do you see in Rahab?

Chapter 3

A Question Of Control

(Don't Lose Control of YOUR Garden!)
Genesis Chapter 3

It's always been a question of control. The strategy of the enemy battles with you by trying to control your thought life. So it was in the Garden of Eden. The 'Let There Be's' were done and God said, "Let Us". God created male and female, blessed them and placed them in a beautiful garden. Having been kicked out of heaven, Satan set out to control humans and their garden. His tactic has not changed. He aims to control your mind and thus control your destiny.

As we move toward our destiny, God gives us provision, instructions and consequences. These help us to conquer the challenges we will meet as we live out our destiny. When God placed Adam in the garden He told him to care for the garden. His instructions were, "You may eat freely of every tree of the garden; but of the tree of the knowledge of good and evil, for in the day that you eat it, you shall die." So many people see the garden of Eden as a paradise where there were no cares, but in every situation of blessing there is always challenge that will determine who is in control. Adam had work to do. He had to till the garden, live in obedience and lead his family into obedience.

Do you understand the dilemma of the adversary? Do you realize that when you receive a blessing from God the enemy sets out to control it? The enemy's access road to control in your situation begins by gaining control of your mind or the mind of someone close to you. That's why the Apostle Paul advises us in Romans 12 to be transformed or changed by the renewing of our minds. We must face it! The devil is after the mind. We must stand in the gap for those who wrestle with the enemy for control of their mind.

Mis-Directed

"And when the woman saw that the tree was good for food, and that it was a delight to the eyes, and that the tree was to be desired to make one wise, she took of the fruit thereof, and did eat; and she gave also unto her husband with her, and he did eat." Gen 3:6 ASV

Who can trace the history of woman without saying that God in His creativity touched this world with gentleness and loveliness, strength and wisdom, virtue and honor and called her woman. In the book of Genesis, we learn the sacred record of God's special creation (1:26,27; 2:18-24). We were patterned after God Himself, made to rule with Adam, blessed and made stewards, then given the charge to multiply and fill the earth. From the beginning, we were made for companionship and partnership. The better we understand ourselves, the more fully we can live out God's purpose for our lives. Even though we were wonderfully made, our purpose sustained a blow in that Eve was mis-directed by Satan.

How quickly she had forgotten the three tenets of her own confession (vs. 3), "...but God did say, 'You must not eat fruit from the trees in the garden, and you must not touch it, or you will die'." What causes us to listen to the offer of Satan and forget the promises of God? Satan had convinced Eve that disobedience to God would make her wise. He caught her alone without her male counterpart and devised to sabotage the plan of God for humanity through deception.

Satan twisted God's instruction not to eat of the tree in the midst of the garden and His reason for the prohibition. We must remember that the wisdom of God is far greater than the wisdom of men. It is our desire to be women of understanding who affect our families and the world around us in a positive way. God has placed in us influence. Adam was more inclined to listen to Eve than he was to listen to God because women are persons of influence. We have both wisdom and intuition. We must raise our sons and daughters to listen to God first.

Our inclination is to nurture rather than neglect, to build rather than tear down. Every woman is different. Not all have the same gifts, dreams or desires. All of us have potential, all have purpose.

Though imperfect as are all humans, we must never forget that every day we are given can be the first day of the rest of our lives. In building others, we must remember to build ourselves and to attach ourselves to those who will build us up rather than tear us down.

There Is A Man In Every Boy

"You have a gift of God, an inner fire..." 2 Timothy 1:6
Study 1st and 2nd Timothy

One of the most powerful relationships in the New Testament is the father-son bond between Paul and Timothy. The attachment between them serves to encourage Timothy as he grows through the natural life stages of maturity. By sharing his short comings and giving Timothy the benefit of his own experience, Paul adds commonality to their relationship. He positions himself to help the man inside Timothy to develop. Timothy is God's vessel but in order for him to operate at his best, transition must take place to position him for the call of God on his life. And so, Paul takes on the awesome responsibility of mentoring.

It was a point of growth in Paul's life and becomes a point of growth in your life when you realize that you cannot accomplish God's purpose in the world alone but you must mentor others. Paul and Timothy were not blood relatives, yet Paul refers to him as "my son." Although Timothy had not reached maturity and had some ways that were boyish, Paul knew that there was a man inside Timothy, ripe for molding. Reaching the man inside the boy is a one on one link through which we touch lives one at a time. It is, in fact, the aim and commitment of Christians to touch individuals on a personal level—one at a time. Paul tells Timothy, "I laid hands on you and blessed you." To fully understand this process you must tap into what Paul refers to as "the spirit of adoption." (Romans 8:15)

In the Greco-Roman meaning of this phrase, a person who is not naturally a part of the family is grafted, placed, or implanted into the family as if they were a natural part of it. And so Paul plants a part of his zeal, his passion, his love and devotion to Christ into the heart of young Timothy and becomes his guide through the rough places. Partnering with God to develop individuals is a slow process, and many times some people become more concerned about the crowd than the development of the individual. You have to ask yourself if your commitment to this life is to only feed the masses or has

God called you to bring out the man in some young Timothy—to patiently develop the one as you feed the masses.

Paul had a Timothy, a Barnabas, and a Silas. Men, you must not let the world mold our young men. God has placed young men all around you that have great potential within. They just need your nurturing and guidance to bring it out. Who better than you to partner with God to develop the boy into a man? Paul could have stood back and said, "Look at the mess Timothy is making." Read the record. The apostle Paul committed his prayer life to Timothy that he be blessed. I can see him never closing a prayer before he asked God to bless Timothy.

He reminded him of the investment God had made in him through his mother Eunice and grandmother Lois. He told Timothy he must invest in his own purpose and gave him life principles to live by. Growing up is tough. It's hard to transition from a boy to a man. You've been there. You question your ability, your worth and your identity. Partner with God to help young men through this unstable period of their lives. Some of you have a call on your life from God to reach out to men who missed their season of nurturing as a boy. Although they are now mature in age, they are still in need of someone to bring out the man that's in the boy. You are God's man called to touch lives one life at a time, to bring out the man that's in the boy.

The Flow From Your Life

"Whoever believes in me...streams of living water shall flow from within him..." John 7:38

On the last day of the feast of Tabernacles (Lev. 23:33), Jesus made an announcement, "if you believe... "What a word! You're probably wondering, as I did, when God showed me this word. What can flow from my innermost being to meet the need of someone else when I sometimes feel so powerless in my own personal situation?

The feast of Tabernacles was the third of seven of the annual Jewish celebrations. The first two are Passover and Pentecost. This feast is symbolic of the fullness of heaven on the earth. It is what Peter alluded to when he wanted to build three tabernacles on the mountain of Transfiguration (Matthew 17:4). This announcement by Jesus is so interesting because He is speaking of the power they would have after He had sent the Holy Spirit. It is the power we have after receiving the Holy Spirit. Isn't it just like Jesus? He is speaking in faith about what they will do after they receive the promise.

It is what He has done for us. He has spoken that we will receive power and that we will be effective because of it. We are mighty children of God filled with His precious promise. Out of our innermost being shall flow rivers of what brings life. Out of our brokenness shall flow rivers of wholeness. Out of our poverty shall flow rivers of wealth. Out of our sickness shall flow rivers of healing because we are a people of faith who believe in Jesus. The power of our faith brings life and healing and deliverance when we find our place in the plan of God through faith and intercession.

What we fill our life with determines what will flow from our lives. Be filled with His hope, His promise, and His power. Allow Christ to fill you, then say what Jesus says about you. Out of your innermost being shall flow rivers of what brings life. This speaks of possession. Out of our possession, His gift, the Holy Spirit, shall flow rivers of water. This is a powerful promise from our powerful Lord to a power filled people.

This is a powerful commitment that Christ has made to us. We will not be empty or powerless but there is a flow of energy from glory that flows through us to those who we pray for, lay hands on and speak life into.

The Value of the Mind

Genesis 3:1-5

What is the mind? Is it like the brain, a mass that has many compartments, with neurons and synapses? Or is it something much larger and deeper? When exploring the mind, the answers that we look for can sometimes seem so abstract. But allow me, by the power of the Holy Spirit, to remove the elusiveness of the mind.

We will discuss what the mind is and the value that both God and the enemy attribute to the mind. The mind can be defined as the seat of perception and understanding. This definition can also be linked to our memories. Although ideas of what defines the mind differ, we are, for the most part, focusing on the decision making facet of a person. Impressions, influence, inner thoughts, desires, feelings, a conglomerate of things cause us to make decisions and change them. We generally speak of this as making up and changing our minds.

The mind is valuable to the enemy because it is God's creation that influences the will. God allows us to have free will, but the mind is the control center. If the mind has not been transformed, if we leave the mind to be influenced by the flesh rather than being changed by the Spirit of God, we have given way for Satan to set up residence in the control center. That's why we are admonished by the apostle Paul in Romans (12) not to be conformed to this world but rather be transformed, be changed from the state in which we were born—that is, born in sin, shaped in iniquity.

The flesh is exposed to fleshly things then the mind begins to churn and either accepts or rejects the exposure to carnality. This is the soil where the agnostic seed breeds and flourishes also. Cults take carnal knowledge to prey upon young people today. More than ever, we are a generation who has been pressed to be educated. We were exposed to theories like Darwinism in classrooms that made light of Creationism. This same so called "enlightened" generation has been taught to place the knowledge of man above the knowledge of God. No wonder this generation is such a breeding ground for deception. Before I take you too much deeper, let us go into our text lesson.

Now in this text lesson we find that the serpent, Satan, is having a discussion with Eve about what God told Adam. The serpent asked Eve, "Can it really be that God said that you shall not eat of every tree in the garden?" (Genesis 3) This is a very crafty trick that the devil is feeding God's people with today. How? Listen to the question. 'Can it really be that God said? Maybe you mis-understood.' What the enemy was really trying to do was to make Eve reason the answer to the question in her mind. Satan was basically asking, 'Does this make sense?'

The commandments, the edicts, the ways of God can never be understood with the mind only by revelation from the Holy Spirit into our spirits. The Holy Spirit must interpret, reveal or open up the will of God to our minds. Let's go deeper. The Bible goes on to say that Eve responded to the enemy, "We can eat from every tree in the garden except from the one in the middle for if we eat from that one we will surely die." (Genesis 3) This is the point where the people of God get into trouble. Immediately, when we are told something that comes against what God has said and the mind begins to churn and chew on or reject the exposure, we need to close our ears to the devils lies. Instead of cutting the enemy down at the pass, we try to have a long drawn out discussion with him, something we were never told to do. We are actually told to "cast down every imagination or argument that rises up against the knowledge of Jesus Christ." (2 Corinthians 10:5)

Whenever the enemy tries to make you reason in your mind what God said and you don't cast him out, you open the door for the ultimate deception.

Let's go deeper. Let's apply this to every day life. The truth of the matter is that this is much like situations that the people of God might find themselves in. Satan enters our territory. Notice Eve didn't go to Satan, he came to her and challenged everything God had told her. Adam was pastor and Eve was first lady in the garden. You would have thought they were too rooted to listen. But the enemy began to work with their minds and cause them to question the rationale and authority of God. He began to challenge the idea that God had their best interest at heart. This is what he does today.

For example, in the text lesson Eve was driven by hunger and questions in her mind. You might be driven by the pursuit of a mate. What God does is simple. The scripture in Psalm 27 says that if you delight yourself in the Lord, He will give you the desires of your heart. When you were saved, God removed the 'old man' desire and implanted His will for your life in your heart. So when you pray and say "Lord, I desire a mate," God says, "Good, that's what I desire for your life." Meanwhile, the Lord is preparing you and your mate for each other. While this process is taking place, the enemy rises up and says, "You want a mate? I can give you one." The enemy also says, "See how long you have been waiting on God to supply you with a mate? God has taken all this time and still what you desire has not taken place yet. Let me handle this." Do you see what the devil is attempting to do?

First he is telling you that God does not want you to have what you desire and secondly that God has taken too long. See, the devil's method has not changed but his question has. Instead of asking if God is really telling you the truth he says, "What do _you_ want? What is _your_ will?" God, through his Spirit, is molding us into what He wants us to be. The scripture says in Romans 12:2, "Be ye not conformed to this world but be ye transformed by the renewing of your mind. So that ye may prove what is that good, acceptable, and perfect will of God." It is only by the renewing of our minds in the word of God that we can have the perfect will of God take place in our lives. God uses this renewing to help us crave His will. The enemy tries to make us crave our own will. God uses His still small voice to plead with us and convince us to do it His way.

Although, the enemy knows that every word of God is true, he tries to make people reason the word of God with their minds. Under this reasoning, if something makes sense, then it is true, but anything that doesn't make sense is not true. This is the understanding that Eve operated under in this passage. She went up to the tree. The fruit looked good to eat. So to her, what God said did not make sense. Satan was playing with her mind. Don't let the devil play with your mind. Stand on what you know about God.

Healing For The Mind, The Body and The Soul

Malachi 4:2, Luke 8:2,3

Both the prophet Malachi and the evangelist Luke recognized the need for spiritual healing. Malachi preached to Judah to confront a people who had gotten off track, relapsed into old habits, old lifestyles, and old patterns of sin. Luke sought to reveal a Savior who healed with a touch. Both of these God fearing men announced that the solution to your healing is to get into the presence of God. You need to know today that there is spiritual healing for the mind, the way you think, what you perceive, what you think of yourself, what you think of others, and how you see the world around you. Throughout your life things have happened to shape your mind, your body and your spirit and perhaps some of those things have had a negative effect on you, but we serve a God who heals with His presence. There is healing for your body, the flesh, the part of you that feels physical pain, the part of you that expresses either sin or righteousness. Sin adversely affects our physical bodies but God is a healer of the physical body whether it be cancer or a cold, drugs or alcohol, arthritis or asthma, our God is a healer. He is the healer of the soul, the personality, the very life that God breathed into you, your inner attitude toward God, that which defines your personal existence. All that we are is a loan from God. The body will go back to the dust but the soul will one day stand before God in accountability for what was done with the mind and the body. Genesis 2:7 says that God formed man of the dust of the ground and breathed into his nostrils the breath of life and man became a living soul. Without the breath of God, mankind was just a lump of clay. You are a living soul that never dies because you are God-breathed. God breathed into man the will, the mind and the emotions. All three, are powerful tools that can either be controlled by flesh or the Holy Spirit. If you allow the Holy Spirit to control your mind, your will, and your emotions, you will get godly results. If you allow the flesh to control your mind, your will, and your emotions, you will get fleshly results. Things that man allows to set up residence in the soul makes the soul a candidate for healing. The soul is the vacuum, the space of God that He gives us permission through our decisions to fill with evil or good but the soul can be healed. While hurt or pain in the physical body can be controlled by medicine, hurt and pain in the spirit and the emotions can only be healed by the Holy Spirit. Healing begins with acknowledgement, that is, the confession that your soul came from the very breath of God and you want Him to fill it with Himself, His power, and His presence. The second step is accountability. It is your decision to let God heal your soul and healing of the soul is healing of the mind and the body. The third step is responsibility. Position yourself to be healed. Make some life changing decisions. Get into the word. Surround yourself with godly, like minded people. Fight what Paul called the good fight of faith. Don't do what the devil tells you just because He attacks your mind. Determine not to wallow in the past and make excuses for yourself because you've been through something. Everyone has been through something. You may not have had a choice in what you have been through, but you do have a choice as to how you will allow it to affect you. There is healing for the mind, the body, and the soul.

Think On These Things

"Finally, brethren, whatsoever things are true, whatsoever things are honest, whatsoever things are just, whatsoever things are pure, whatsoever things are lovely, whatsoever things are of good report: If there be any praise (anything praiseworthy), think on these things." Philippians 4:8

In this letter, Paul is advising us on our thought life. God monitors the thought life of A Christian. The thoughts are important because thoughts are the birthplace of our actions. Proverbs 23:7 teaches us that as a man thinks in his heart, so is he. Thinking begins the thought process and thinking determines the state of the spirit and of the attitude. Thinking precedes what is spoken. Good or bad habits are but seeds planted in the thought process that manifest themselves in our actions. So then, the Apostle Paul admonishes that thoughts should be filled with honesty, fairness, purity, loveliness and good reports.

We are living in a time when there is so much influence on our thought life. The reports we hear on the news do not build a productive thought life. Man has gone from one level of heinous crimes to another. The newspaper and many times the conversation we share with others are not faith based. But if we train our minds according to the scripture, our lives will have the foundation to produce fruit that is kingdom building.

What an impact we could have on the world if we could spiritually nourish our thought life to the point that we are on automatic. Our mouth opens and we plant seeds of encouragement automatically as we speak. The harvest of a good thought life is a good testimony. Your life planted in a world of heartache becomes a seed that springs forth with words that bind the broken heart, a seed that gives hope where there is despair. Take the challenge. Nourish your mind on," whatsoever things are true, whatsoever things are honest, whatsoever things are just, whatsoever things are pure, whatsoever things are lovely, whatsoever things are of good report: If there be any praise (anything praiseworthy), think on these things." Philippians 4:8

Questions for Discussion

Chapter Three
It's A Question of Control
(Don't Lose Control Of YOUR Garden!)

Section One
Mis-Directed

1. Has Satan ever tried to derail the plan of God for your life?
2. In most situations, we have hindsight. We say what might have been done? What advice would you give Eve?

Section Two
There Is A Man In Every Boy

1. What natural stages do we go through that we sometimes fail to share?
2. Think about a person you know that you might mentor. What possibilities do you see in him or her?

Section Three
The Flow From Your Life

1. Think about an experience that has greatly affected you. What did God cause to come out of that experience that has caused a flow in your life?

Section Four
The Value of the Mind

1. Why is the mind so valuable? To Satan? To God? How do we see this in the world today?
2. What should we do with knowledge that rises against the knowledge of Jesus Christ?
3. What is the difference between conforming and being transformed?

Section Five
Healing For Mind, Body and Soul

1. Are we sometimes more aware of physical illness than spiritual illness?
2. What is the difference between accountability and responsibility?

Section Six
Think On These Things

1. How does your thought life effect our actions?
2. How can your thoughts affect others?

Chapter 4

Cultivating A Revelation Testimony

I thank God for the teaching of my parents. When I was growing up we were not allowed to use language they did not use. Consequently, profanity and slang was not welcome in our home. If we said something that was slang or profane my mother's first question was, "Is this something you've heard me or your dad say?" That was all she needed to say to let us know it was unacceptable. As we grew, we learned that we should speak only what the word of God said over our lives. Of course, this was a very valuable lesson. Too often, we don't practice that teaching from the word. If you want to move forward in God, and if you want to embrace your tomorrow today, you must learn to cultivate a revelation testimony. That is, speak what God has shown you rather than what you see. A revelation testimony is the firm foundation that makes you hold onto what God has said when all around you seems to be shaking. A revelation testimony is developed based upon reading the promises of God but you must go a step further and spend time with God so that He can open the promise in your spirit. Something happens on the inside of you when God reveals His promise to you. Confidence builds. Anointing grows. Revelation is the oil that puts a burning in you just as oil in a lamp brings fire. You have to allow God to light up your life with His revealing power. That's the light that will bring people out of darkness. Begin to see what God has spoken over your life. You are a lender, not a debtor. You are the head and not the tail. You have His peace. You are His light in this world. You are already a teacher, already an architect, already a mother, already a doctor. There is a line that separates those who move according to what God has shown them (revelation) and those who move according to their circumstance. Abraham's body said it was old and too dead to produce life, but God said nothing is too hard for Him (Genesis 18:14). Revelation knowledge is that vehicle mixed with faith that will take you from promise to manifestation. Revelation knowledge will take you from the prayer of faith to the point of receiving what you have believed. You need to read the word. You need Bible study. You need the preaching and teaching of the word, but you personally need to spend time with God so that He can plant a revelation word in your spirit. This will convince you to the point that you will not be moved in your storms, but you will be like a tree with deep roots. You will be, as Colossians says (2:6) rooted and built up in Christ and established in the faith.

From The Pasture To The Palace

2 Samuel 7:8b

I want to talk about David and how we as believers go from our season of being a shepherd to being in a season of kingship. When we think about how long we've been in our individual fields as shepherds, can we believe that it's our season to emerge out of the pastures of life, fighting bears and lions and move into kingship? 2 Samuel 7:8b says, "I took you from the pasture, from following the sheep, to be prince over my people in Israel." So how did David go from the pasture to the palace? Join me in 1 Samuel 16:1-13.

The first thirteen verses are dedicated to showing the reader how David was anointed. The first king of Israel, Saul had disobeyed God. Samuel, God's prophet, was grieving over the fact that God had decided to tell Saul to step down as king of Israel. God told Samuel to fill his horn with oil and go to the home of Jesse, the Bethlehemite, because there was a king among his sons. In obedience to God, Samuel went to Jesse's home. He looked at each son just waiting to know God's choice for the next king. Samuel invited Jesse and his sons to join him in sacrificing to the Lord. David was not invited, yet he was God's choice. Jesse made seven of his sons pass before Samuel, but none of them was God's choice. As Samuel looked at each one, God's message to him was "man looks at the outward appearance, but God looks at the heart." (vs. 7) Samuel looked at the height and good looks of each son and all the time God was rejecting them. You may not be man's choice, but God chooses people He can develop. Man looks at the finished product while God looks at raw material. Man looks in the mirror and God looks upon the soul. God looks at the inner man and the intent of the heart. God looks at the willingness of a yielded heart. God has appointed a place for you to rule, a place for you to be the head and not the tail. You are a star that He wants to use to light some path. How will you get from your pasture to your kingship? Someone may step in line ahead of you. They may beat you to the interview, but it's God's promise to you. Your blessing cannot pass you by. Samuel asked Jesse if he had any other sons. Jesse said, 'Yes, but he is out watching the sheep.' Can you imagine? He was the youngest. He was the new kid on the block. Samuel instructed them to go get David. He said they would not sit down until David arrived. God held up the party until David came. When God has prepared your space nothing can happen until you get there. Your destiny is reserved for you. David was the least of his brothers. He was not considered to be the one most likely to succeed. He was not even where most people would consider the place of blessing, yet He was God's choice. The journey for a king was from the shepherd field. God's choice for a king was not based upon the build of the body but the condition of his heart. David's testimony would always be that he was a shepherd for a season, then God anointed him king. David was a shepherd boy, a musician, a saint, a sinner, a prophet and a king, but most of all, he was a man whose heart God looked upon and said, "Arise, anoint him; for this is he." (1 Samuel 16:12) This helps me to move forward in my destiny because when it looks like things are not happening fast enough or if I feel stuck in time, I remember how God took David from the pasture to the palace.

Trusting God With Our Seed

*"So he took him home, and his mother held him on her lap;
...She carried him up to the bed of the prophet and shut the door."*
2 Kings 4:8-37

One of the most difficult decisions a parent makes is knowing how and when to turn their children loose. Children need space to grow and develop and move on to maturity. They need the space to form other relationships and most importantly their own relationship with God. We are privy to the experience of a woman in this very situation. She has come to be called the Shunamite woman. This woman who lived with her husband came to know Elisha the prophet by being kind to him. She first invited him to dinner when he had come to town. Later she asked her husband to build a room for him so he could be comfortable whenever he passed through as he ministered in their town. This woman was unable to have children and Elisha prophesied that she would birth a son within the next year. After the child was born, he had a sun stroke and died. This mother asked her husband to send one of the servants with a donkey to take her to the prophet of God. All along the way she was questioned. All of her answers were responses in faith. Her son was covered in faith as he awaited the miracle of God. She was committed to the life of her son. So it is with us. We must cover our children in faith. We must be committed to teaching them to have a strong walk with God. Our children have so many more challenges than we had. Some of them forced into behavior that they do not even desire. We must pray and confess the will of God over their lives. Just as the Shunamite woman refused to leave Elisha until he dealt with her son's challenge, we must stay on our face before God for the deliverance of our children. Our children must matter enough for us to drop everything we are doing to come to their rescue. To turn loose our children is the safe thing to do when we release them into the loving arms of Christ, but we cannot afford to turn them loose into the hands of the enemy. How much do you love your children? Are they important enough to hold on to until you can release them into the hands of God?

Where There Is Unity, There Is Strength!

Philippians

The book of Philippians is a wonderful book for family Bible study whether it is the church family or your own personal family. This book has so much to say about the power of a unified family. If ever there was a time for unity in the family, whether it is in your home or the church family, it is now. We know that Satan's tactic is to divide and conquer. God values unity and brings about strength through it. Paul teaches us that where there is unity there is consolation, comforting love, fellowship and compassion. Paul sets Christ-like humility and love as the cornerstone of unity. This book is medicine on the battleground learn from the apostle Paul, the teacher of this Philippians community?

His tone is one of love. He opens this letter with the tender love of a spiritual father. As you read this letter, you know instantly that he is addressing a need in this church family. This was a church family who was close to Paul's heart. God had begun a good work in them and Paul had faith that God would complete it. They supported him in missionary work. This church had such an availing prayer life that it brought about deliverance, but the church had a problem. There was division. Some of it centered around Syntyche and Euodia. Notice that Paul does not ignore the need or run away from the problem. He addresses it, identifies the source and gives the remedy. Paul knew that unity would not only be healing to these two Christian women, but it would also heal those who followed them. Perhaps there is a need for unity in your home, your church family or community. The answer is in Philippians.

In chapter 2, real unity is expressed in *consolation*. Here the Greek is actually interpreted, "exhortation or encouragement; to be like minded." When a member of the family, congregation or community has a tendency toward selfishness or conceit, it is the duty of others to encourage them to act in love and humility. The second contributor to unity is a certain comfort of *love*. This is the God kind of love that stimulates others to be like-minded. Love causes us to care when there is discord. It makes us resist division and urge one another to have peace in the family. The third aspect is that there is a spirit of *fellowship*. Of course, when there is encouragement and love in the family this promotes fellowship. The family will feel bound together. Although circumstances and trials may differ, although under different roofs, there is a bond that says, "We're in this together." Family members have a common relationship and a common goal and that is for the well being of all. There is a ministry of the spirit that glues family members together. Finally, there are "*bowels of mercy*" that unify the family. Bowels refer to the heart. There are compassionate yearnings that come from the heart. There is a saying. I don't know where I first heard or read it but the words are meaningful. I reinforce these words in our home and our church. "We are a family. We need one another. We love one another. We forgive one another. We work together. We play together. We worship together. Together we use God's word. Together we love all mankind. Together we serve our God. Together we hope for heaven." Where there is unity, there is strength!

Remember Mama

St John 19:26,27

The noise of the crowd could not overshadow her pain. She could hear the ringing of the hammer as they nailed her son to the cross. Her eyes, for a time, focused upon the soldiers' spear that riveted His side. Mocking words from the crowd demanded that He save Himself as He had saved others. These words pulled on her heart as she, in flashback fashion, remembered the many things she had held in her heart over the years.

No doubt Mary remembered the Wise Men bringing gifts that were fit for a king when he was a newborn baby, fleeing to Egypt to save His life when Herod declared a baby massacre, finding Him in the temple when He left the security of the caravan returning home from worship, all the miracles, the healings, the ties that bound her to her Son, Jesus the Christ. Suddenly, above the noise of the crowd, she heard the words, "Woman behold, (see) your son. Son, behold, (see) your mother." Jesus, our Lord, remembered His mother. He made sure that she would not have to face life alone. Determined to do the right thing for His mother as a son, Jesus made the decision to leave her in the care of someone He knew would love her just as He did. John would take Mary as his own mother. Can you imagine the special privilege and responsibility John felt standing at the cross when Jesus revealed to John the incredible trust He had in his friend? Nothing else had ever pulled Jesus away from His mission, but this time, Jesus had to stop dying long enough to remember His mother. Through many years of ministry, I've heard so many people in remorse, realizing that mama is now with God resting from her labor, yet wishing they could hear their mother's voice and experience her touch of tenderness one more time. Let me tell you that now is the time to "Remember Mama." Now is the time to remind her how much you love her, appreciate her labor of love, stand ready anytime to do for her, and constantly remind her how important she is in your life. There is nothing like the relationship between a mother and child. No matter how old you are and what responsibilities you have gained, the presence of mother allows you to pull away from the harshness of this life and rest securely in her love. I've got to tell you today that I truly thank God for my mother every new morning I am blessed to open my eyes. Mother Maggie B. Yates of Mobile, Alabama I believe is the perfect picture of what God intended those who are blessed to be called mothers to walk like. She is the proud mother of nine children, of which I am number five the centerpiece, and she has always had enough love to give to each of us. I treasure her tenderness and her wisdom, her ability to look beyond my imperfections and still love me. I can hear her say, even as I pen these words, "God knew what I needed when He gave me my children." Don't miss this precious moment God has given you to remember Mama.

Maturity

"Don't let anyone think little of you because you are young. Be their ideal; (example) let them follow the way you teach and live; be a pattern for them in your love, your faith and your clean thoughts." 1 Timothy 4:12

Maturity means to grow and to develop. God wants young people to grow spiritually, mentally and physically. As you grow, He wants your lives to be an example to others. Many people think that maturity is about age, but maturity has to do with growth. Some people who are very young are more mature than some people who are very old. There are three things I want you to remember about maturity.

1. *A mature person has the right attitude about the past.*

   Both good and bad experiences are a part of everyone's life. A mature person thanks God for the good things in the past and looks for opportunities to be a blessing to others. Ask God to heal painful experiences and use them as stepping stones to climb higher in life.

2. *A mature person has the right attitude about the present.*

   A person that is growing and developing knows that they are responsible for the present. God has given you this special time in your life and you have the responsibility of making the most of it.

3. *A mature person has the right attitude about the future.*

God has a plan for your future. The best way to prepare is to make sure God is first in your life. Seek the guidance of God each day. He knows how to direct you so that you are ready for your future.

Build Your Life On Jesus!

"For no other foundation can anyone lay than that which is laid, which is Jesus Christ." 1 Corinthians 3:11

One of the most important things in life is to have a good foundation. I mean, every where you go, people have their opinions about things, so you pretty much need to already know what you believe. A foundation is what something is built on. It supports that which is built. The most important foundation is what we build our lives on. That is why Paul wrote this very important letter to the people in Corinth. They were a young church whose members were trying to build a life for themselves. They were growing up in Christ. Paul reminded them to build their lives on Jesus. It was a very important time in their lives and how they built their lives was very important.

This is a very important time in your life, and how you build your life is important. All the things you learn and do now will determine what your life will be like as an adult. God loves you! He wants you to build your life on Jesus. There are many decisions ahead of you, but if you put Jesus first in your life. He will lead you through them. You will be deciding who you will marry and the kind of work you will do. You are, in fact, making those decisions now by the friends you choose and what you learn in school. If you pick friends who don't love Jesus, you might fall in love with one of them and marry the wrong person. If you learn all you can in school, there will be more jobs for which you will qualify. Your friends, who you will marry, your education, and career choices are all very important. These things are a part of life, but you should not build your life on them. Your friends will come and go. What you like to do as a hobby or a career may change. You want to build your life on someone who can take you through the good and bad times in life. Take the challenge! BUILD YOUR LIFE ON JESUS!

Questions for Discussion

Chapter Four
Cultivating A Revelation Testimony

Section One
From The Pasture To The Palace

1. What is your pasture to palace story?
2. What message is God speaking to your situation through this lesson?

Section Two
Trusting God With Our Seed

1. Write about or discuss an experience in which you had trouble trusting God with your seed.

Section Three
Where There Is Unity...There Is Strength!

1. What is your relationship like with your spiritual father? (Paul was the spiritual father to those in the church.)
2. What are your unrealized dreams and are you confident that God will not leave them unfulfilled?
3. What is God speaking to you about your family situation? Both spiritual and natural families, be specific.

Section Four
Remember Mama

1. Write about or discuss an experience you had with your mother. It can be a special memory. To those who grew up without a mother what are some of the motherly experiences that God has allowed you to have?

Section Five
Maturity

1. Who is looking at you as their example?
2. What are some ways in which God can use you in shaping those who are patterning themselves after you?

Section Six
Build Your Life On Jesus

1. What are some things that you can do to make sure your foundation and your relationship with Jesus stays strong?

Chapter 5

God Has Prepared You For Your Battle

Matthew 4:1-11

I want to talk to you about the temptation of Jesus in the desert. What is a desert? It is a hot, dry, and unbearable place. For some a desert is in their mind. It's the place where the devil attacks, but Jesus put the devil in his place! In this situation, Jesus was sent by the Holy Spirit to be tempted by the enemy. Before I go on, know that God will never place you in a situation that He has not prepared you for. So Jesus was led by the Holy Spirit to face a battle in which God had already prepared Him to be victorious. He went without food. He was fasting. Why would Jesus have to fast? I mean, He's Jesus! Think with me… Could it be that, He was showing us how to face our battles? Jesus had an answer for every challenge Satan made. Every word of God Jesus had hidden in His heart was for a purpose. God had been preparing Him for this battle His whole life. Guess what? Every word of God we learn is preparing us for the battles we will face now and in the future. We must prepare before we are in battle. The enemy told Jesus to turn stones into bread. Jesus had His word ready, Matthew 4:4, "Man shall not live by bread alone but by every word that proceedeth out of the mouth of God." He refused to be tempted to satisfy the flesh because His spirit was more important. So now we know what to do when Satan tries to tempt us on the level of the flesh. The next thing the enemy did was try to get Jesus to glorify himself rather than God. He wanted Jesus to be hungry for attention. It is a trick the enemy still tries to play on the children of God. He wants us to try to take the credit for what God does in our lives. The devil tried to get Jesus to end it all. 'If you are as important to God as you say you are, put yourself in harms way. Jump from the roof of the church. Can't you hear the devil, "Jump Jesus jump! I can hear Jesus….." Man, you must be crazy! Actually, Jesus said, "it is written also, you shall not tempt the Lord your God." The devil tries yet again to stop Jesus from winning His battle. From a very high mountain, the enemy shows Jesus the riches of the world and tries to offer Him something that Jesus already owned. What is the devil thinking... offering Jesus the kingdoms of the earth? The enemy offered Him these things in exchange for worship. Again, Jesus said no. He told the enemy, "It is written, you shall worship the Lord your God and only Him." After that, the devil departed from Jesus and angels came and ministered to Him. This was a big one because God created us to worship Him. Even in the Old Testament when God told Moses to tell Pharaoh to let His people go, the purpose of their freedom was to worship Him (Exodus 5:1-3). Our worship belongs only to God. Just as God sent angels to minister to Jesus, in our daily lives, whenever we've been beaten down, God always sends someone to minister to or encourage us. This Matthew 4:1-11 scripture is a great passage to read, especially when you are going through something. It is a reminder that not only is God with you but Jesus has gone though the same thing victoriously. As I close, remember that Jesus didn't let the devil have His mind, God will never allow you to go through something He has not prepared you for, and God is with you wherever you go.

How Can I Be Strong

2 Chronicles 28:12
"All riches and wealth come from you;
you rule everything by your strength and power;
and you are able to make anyone great and strong."

As I was praying for you, God showed me a people facing difficult situations who want to be strong. Like David you have had some experience with God. You have seen Him provide for you in tough times and bring strength in your spirit for the battles you face. These are challenging times and God has a message of strength for those facing battles that seem to come one after another. God has a word for you. He is your source of strength. Experience with God gives you confidence in God. You have learned that the power of God is released on your behalf. As God did with David in this passage, He enters your battle and substitutes His strength for your weakness. Your failures give opportunity for His success. The books of 1st and 2nd Chronicles cover the same history that 1st and 2nd Samuel and 1st and 2nd Kings cover. The difference is that the Chronicles are specifically about David, God's king. Just as David was God's king and God's ambassador of authority over Israel, you are God's ambassador in your situation. He has placed you where you are to give you victory. In the Chronicles you learn about the obedience and victory of David as well as the disobedience and times of defeat. They help you because through his battles you learn how to deal with the spiritual warfare that you engage in. You, too, are rulers and kings over that which God gives you charge. You engage in spiritual warfare to protect that kingdom. You can learn to have victory through God's spiritual principles. David knew that his God was strong and mighty in battle and had the ability to make him strong and mighty in battle. Why was David able to make such a powerful proclamation? *All* riches and wealth come from God! God rules *everything* by His strength and power! He is able to make *anyone* great and strong! He had experienced it! He knew that the blessing of God follows the submissive heart. He had learned and even taught his son Solomon to trust God (Proverbs 3:6). God had taken David from victory over a lion and a bear (1 Samuel 17:34-35), to victory over a Philistine giant. He had taken him from the cave of Abdullah to the throne (1 Samuel 22:1). David was strong. He had a strength that had nothing to do with his size, his money or his education. You too can be strong. How can you be strong? Trust God enough to have a real relationship with Him. Allow Him to direct your steps daily. Pray and ask God for direction, then listen for His voice of guidance. Strength comes to those who trust in the power of God's might (Eph. 6:10). Be strong when the enemy comes in like a flood because your God will raise a standard against him(Isa. 59:19). Be strong when your mind tells you that you are weak because God is the strength of your life (Psa. 27:1).

There's Never Enough Time!

Matthew 6:25-34

    I know for me, it always feels like there's never enough time in a day for me to get everything done. I make a list as soon as I get up and determine not to start my day worrying about how I will accomplish my goals. My time is limited and valuable, so how do I make the most of it? Prioritize. I put God first. Matthew 6:25-34 says, "Do not worry about what you shall eat, what you shall drink, or what you shall wear. God knows you need these things and He will take care of them for you. Seek Him first and He will supply you with all these things as well." He's got me covered and He's got you covered too! Prioritizing is not something you can figure out on your own. You need the Holy Spirit to lead you. God is a God of order (1 Corinthians 14:40). He doesn't want you to live your life haphazardly. So, you ask God for guidance in your decision-making. You make it a habit to pray to God the first thing in the morning and throughout the day to get His direction. God always delivers (Matthew 7:7-8).

God's Priorities

1. _____
2. _____
3. _____
4. _____
5. _____

Follow The Leader

Joshua 1:1-9

I want to talk to you about Moses' successor, Joshua. To get into the text, one question comes to mind. Besides being called by God and exemplifying great faith, what qualified Joshua to lead the Israelites into the promised land?

(1) Joshua was filled with the Spirit of God. In Deuteronomy 34:9, Moses laid hands on Joshua and deposited wisdom from God. Joshua walked closely with Moses and watched his walk with God. It is the plan of God for us to follow in the footsteps that follow Him closely.

(2) Joshua enjoyed the presence of God. Joshua 1:5 was the promise of God that no one could stand against Joshua because God was with him. He had witnessed the power of walking with God through Moses and now was his opportunity.

(3) Joshua was obedient to the will of God. In Joshua 5:14,15, Joshua didn't care how little or big the command was. Joshua obeyed quickly and quietly with everything that was in him.

A leader must be a follower. God has greatness in others that He wants to pass on to you through their example. God has placed his plan and His power in each generation. When we have the humility to receive from those who have come before us we are equipped with double anointing. We have what has been deposited in them and what God has placed in us. For as long as I can remember, I have watched my dad's example and tried to follow it. I thank him for his example. I am also grateful for the example's of my grandfather's the late Deacon Robert L. Yates of Mobile, Alabama and Rev. William A. Bunton, Jr. pastor of the Antioch Baptist Church in Buffalo, New York. Happy Father's Day Dad! Thanks for being a great example. Nothing can replace the example of my mother and granny, First Lady Wanda Bunton, a "shout out" from her favorite grandchild.

Trusting God 101

"When you pass through the waters, I will be with you; and when you pass through the rivers, they will not sweep over you. When you walk through the fire, you will not be burned; the flames will not set you ablaze, says the Lord." Isaiah 43:2

My son lay sick with a 107 degree temperature. I called the doctor. I knew he needed medicine quickly. While my husband went to get the medicine I held him and prayed. The telephone rang. The voice on the other end asked, "Is this the home of a minister?" "Yes," I replied, as I silently continued to pray. I was used to answering telephone calls, praying before I picked up the telephone, saying, "Lord I don't know who's calling or what their need is but give me the words to say." This time I didn't want to pray that prayer. I wanted to take care of my son. The Lord spoke in my spirit, *"You take care of mine and I'll take care of yours."* The voice went on to speak. The lady said she had been young and never gave God a second thought. Now she was old and alone in the world and needed him, but could not ask him for help because it wasn't right to ask God for help when she thought she was too old to give him anything in return. This woman was about to kill herself, but wanted prayer that God would forgive her for taking her life. God had me tell her that His love is not for sale, but His love is free. We don't have to buy it or bargain for it. I went on to minister to her and before we hung up she accepted the Lord Jesus in her heart. When my husband got home he said, 'I'm led to take the baby's temperature before giving him medicine.' God had calmed me down to minister, but I was about to get impatient again. I told him we already knew what his temperature was and nothing had happened to bring it down so I wanted to hurry and give him the medicine. My husband in his slow unassuming way, said, "Well, God is leading me to take his temperature first." I agreed, with the intent of hurrying to get the medicine in him. When we took his temperature there was no fever, it was normal. The voice came back to me, *"You take care of mine and I'll take care of yours."* I began to praise God. After I had emptied in praise, I told my husband all that had happened. He said God had urged him to take our son's temperature first but he didn't know why. He just knew he had to obey. We ministered to this lady for another year. Before we moved to another state, she had joined a church and was baptized. We never met her in person but we know we'll know her in glory. I learned that I would have to release my children to God and trust Him to take them through the waters and fires of life. After all, He was trusting me with His children in ministry. Could I not trust Him with those He had loaned to me? Again and again, I have relied on His faithful promise....*"You take care of mine and I'll take care of yours.'"*

What's A Father To Do?

"There was a man who had two sons. The younger one said to his father, give me my share of the estate. So he divided his property between them. Not long after that the youngest son got together all he had , set off for a distant country and there squandered his wealth in wild living." Luke 15:11-13 (NIV)

Of the four evangelists who set out to help us understand the gospel, Luke consistently makes the divine human connection. He helps his readers get a feel for both the humanity and the divinity of Christ. He showed that Jesus was human, yet he had authority over that which bound humanity. He could heal disease as well as problematic relationships.

You can tell that Luke was a doctor by the way he emphasized the healing ministry of Jesus, how Jesus healed the blind, reached out to the broken, and ministered to those who mourned. He breaks the silence of history and shares all that Jesus began to do and teach (Acts1:1,2). And so Luke helps us to examine spiritual things by using earthly parallels. In Luke 15, he parallels the coin to lost people, a shepherd to the Savior and a lost son to a lost nation. A loving father, a parallel of God Himself, no doubt had poured all of himself into his sons, yet He is confronted with the fact that neither of them wanted to be a family. Their brotherhood was broken just as the brotherhood of the world is broken. How it must break the heart of God to see the nations of the world (His prodigal children) fighting. They are both, in their own way, lost to the plan and purpose of God. The youngest is so bold as to say, 'Give me everything. Though I came into the world with nothing, I want all that you have to give me, then I want to break the ties by moving away from your teaching, your influence, your contribution to who I am and away from your presence.' That is precisely what humanity continues to do to God.

Man is still saying, "Give me everything." Man took all that God had to give and decided to distance himself from God by the lifestyle he chose. Man understood that God is not a hog pen God. Yet man still chose a hog pen lifestyle. God cannot live in the filth of mud, nor eat food prepared for swine.

Millions of Christians stand at the gate of the hog pen of habit, the hog pen of rebellion. Perhaps they are not the ones who eat of the husk themselves, but they are waiting for a loved one to come to themselves. And so Luke's unasked question is, What's a father to do when a loved one turns their back on all that he or she has been taught? What's a father to do with the brokenness in the family?

Both sons had been exposed to the best. They lived in a household where there were fatted calves, royal robes, rings and more than this, love. What's a father to do with one son who is prodigal (wasteful), unappreciative, blind to a fathers' love and the great blessing of the privilege and responsibility of sonship? His other son never left home, but was still a prodigal. The picture Luke paints is perhaps one that you too have experienced. Perhaps you know what it's like to see potential and possibility in someone you love and stand watching as they throw it away.

Possibly you feel powerless as you wait for someone to come to themselves. What can you learn from this father? After having done all to stand, he stood. He gracefully stood by while the son tried his wings. He did not argue with him, but gave him his portion. He continued to be responsible for what God had put him in charge of.

Because of the faithfulness of the father, when the son came to himself there was still a home to return to. He remained open to the direction of God with expectation in his heart. The father was looking for a change when there was no physical evidence that there was a change. When the son was still a long distance away, the father saw him coming.

The son had lost all his money but had found himself. His father was filled with love rather than regret and resentment. The father saw him coming. He ran to his son, embraced him and kissed him.

What's a father to do? He hoped when there was no physical evidence. He forgave both sons before they asked for pardon. He restored one of them while the stench of the hog pen was still on him.

Be a part of God's plan of restoration. Trust God for your loved one to come to himself (or herself). God will not allow you to be disappointed.

"It Took "That!" "

"The Power of A Thank You...I've Got To Say Thank You!"
Romans 8:28; Psalm 100

"And we know that in all things God works for the good of those who love him. who have been called according to his purpose. Romans 8:28

" Shout for joy to the Lord, all the earth. Worship the Lord with gladness; Come before him with joyful songs. Know that the Lord is God.. It is he who made us, and we are his, we are his people, the sheep of his pasture. Enter into his gates with thanksgiving and his courts with praise; give thanks to him and praise his name. For the Lord is good and his love endures forever. Psalms 100

I. The purpose of this message is to speak life to your purpose, your call and your destiny. It is to impart some things into your spirit. This message is to encourage you with some additional thoughts along the way regarding your walk with God.

II. Take a moment to reflect. Close your eyes and think about the first time God revealed to you what He wanted you to do with your life. Think about how you felt, whether you were a young child, a teenager, young adult, or mature adult. Whenever it was, remember the excitement you felt. Now, let that feeling become intense in your spirit. If that feeling has been lost, God wants to let you know that He is "redeeming the time." He is making up for the time you have lost.

In addition, while you are still reflecting, think about what God has done for you up to this point in your life.

Reflect on all the things that God has done for you throughout your life. Reflect on your health, finances and spiritual well being. You know what it is. Begin to reflect. Let that feeling bubble up. Let it resonate. Let it churn in your spirit.

Now, with the way you are feeling, you will better be able to understand what God wants to say in this message.

We will focus on six verses. These verses are powerful.
We will analyze them and extract what God wants us to acquire.

III. <u>The Set-Up:</u> We must remember that in our lives, in our walk with God we are either:

1. In a storm.

2. Coming out of a storm.

3. Going into a storm.

This is important because:

1. It is part of the growth process in your relationship with God.

2. Many times in this process, it requires us to be in a time of isolation. This is good, but to people who are new to the process, it is not understandable. It is frustrating to them. ISOLATION IS SEPERATION FOR PREPARARTION BEFORE ELEVATION. In other words: GOD IS GOING TO "BLOW YOU UP" BIG TIME AND THRUST YOU INTO YOUR PURPOSE AND CALL IN ORDER TO GET YOU TO YOUR DESTINY!

3. The process answers the question, 'I realize my purpose and my destiny , but why do I have to go through the drama and pain in my journey?" Well, you must realize that it helps prepare you and gives you a thankful heart.

What does "that" mean? "It took "that."

Part 1

God said "that" means:

1. That situation or group of situations that you have to go through in your life where you will truly learn about God.

2. That person or group of persons that will come into your life to bring you even closer to God. There are many examples from the Old Testament and the New Testament, which will help you understand the relevancy of what we are learning though this message.

Situation: Abraham and Sarah

God promised Abraham and Sarah a seed, or a son: Genesis 15

God gave a promise to Abraham and Sarah. God gives us promises, which we must impart that promise into our spirit and believe God for it.

The Hagar Factor is introduced and Ishmael is born: Genesis 16

We must not try to help God out. If God said something is going to happen, it's going to happen!

Isaac Is Born: Genesis 21

God's promise came to pass.

Our Mt. Moriah Experiences: Genesis 22

This deals with the fact that when God promises us something, it will come to pass. However, God sometimes tells us to sacrifice the very thing that we were waiting for. We must obey. Abraham offered up Isaac as a sacrifice and in return, God had a ram in the bush. Therefore, Isaac lived.

Situation: Joseph

Joseph was hated for the favor God had on his life: Genesis 37:3-4

His family couldn't handle the dreamer: Genesis 37: 5-6

His brothers handled the dreamer: Genesis 37:18-28

Joseph was prosperous in Potiphar's house: Genesis 39:1-6

He was attacked by Potiphar's wife and put into prison: Genesis 39:7-20

Joseph's favor didn't fail and he still prospered: Genesis 39:21-23

Joseph was transferred from the prison to the palace: Genesis 41

He and his family were re-united: Genesis 43-49

Overall, God blessed Joseph despite all of the "haters to the favor" that he had on his life. Joseph still respected God and was faithful to Him. God then raised him up to a position of great authority.

Situation: David

He was anointed: I Samuel 16:11

David stands up against Goliath: I Samuel 17

David was made king: II Samuel 5

The David, Uriah, and Bathsheba ordeal: II Samuel 11-13

Through all the drama. all the problems that David endured, God did not let it destroy him. He still honored David because, through his lineage, generations later Jesus Christ would come to the world.

Situation: The Widow Woman: I Kings 17

This woman had a period of loss. God gave her back more than she lost. The power of obedience makes things happen. It was a time of "overflow" in her life.

Situation: The Woman with the issue of blood: St. Matthew 9:20; St. Mark 5:25; St. Luke 8:43

This woman was constantly bleeding. The doctors could not help, but made things worse. She had an encounter with Jesus and her situation changed. Jesus can dry up any type of bleeding issue in your life.

Situation: Lazarus: St. John 11:1-44

Lazarus, a friend of Jesus was sick and eventually died. Jesus did not come when Lazarus' sisters beckoned Him. When Jesus did show up, He raised up Lazarus and God was glorified. Jesus can deal with your dead and stinking situations.

Situation: Jesus: Matthew 26:39; 42

Jesus submitted to the will of God. Therefore, salvation was released to all mankind. Jesus had to endure the cross, take on the burdens of the world's sins, although realizing the authority He had. As a result, our relationship with God has been restored. Thank you, Jesus!

Situation: Paul: Acts 9

Paul, was the name God gave Saul when his life was changed. Saul hated Christ and His people, but in the end, he became a mighty man of God. God can change anybody's life. You just have to submit to God's way and He will lead you in the right direction.

We must now bring in the point of Romans 8:28. Paul wrote this scripture. We must realize that everything we experience is all for the greater good, which is to glorify God. We are to be examples for Him. We should not look at our situations as devastating, but as an opportunity for God to work through us. This is why we need to praise God. "I've got to say thank you!" should be the statement that stays in our heart, mind, and soul. Our praise should not be sporadic. It should be consistent!

In support of Psalm 100 , which was written by David, there are other Scriptures that support saying "thank you" through praise unto God. These Scriptures are:

1. Praise for God's providential Care: Psalm 34,35,87,91,107,117, 121,145,146

2. Praise of Thanksgiving: Psalm 9,30,75,116,124,126,135,136

It is the duty of believers in Jesus Christ to realize that there are "haters" of everything, when it is in the will of God. Therefore, we must realize that there are "haters" of the "thank you." In the Word of God we see two spirits that try to destroy or try to keep us from praising the One who needs to be praised.

These spirits are the spirit of:

1. Michal

2. Jezebel

These spirits are dangerous. They will try to bind you up. Believers must take authority when these spirits arise. We can see in the Scripture how these "spirits" were dealt with.

The "spirit" of Michal

Michal was the daughter of Saul. She did not like the fact that David was praising God when the Ark of the Covenant was returned to David's territory. The Ark of The Covenant represented God's presence among the people. Therefore, David put his wife in check. As a result of her action, God did not allow her to have children. (II Samuel 6)

The "spirit" of Jezebel

Jezebel was a wicked queen. She was the wife of King Ahab. Her spirit was a spirit of control, of intimidation. Therefore, that resulted in the end of her life. That brought about her fatal demise.

I Kings 19 1,2: She plans Elijah's death

I Kings 21:23-24: Her death is pronounced

II Kings 9:1-11: Elisha anoints King Jehu and her death is prophesied again

II Kings 30-37: She is killed

These "spirits" must be recognized and there must be an answer back to these demons, when they are manifest. These demon spirits want to bind up your head, your hands, and your feet. Therefore, what shall we do when this happens?

The answer is to hit them with Scriptures. Satan and his demons hate the word of God. Let us apply this, now.

Head:
(Mind) *Psalm 8:9: "We have thought of thy loving kindness O God, in the midst of thy temple."*

Eyes:
Isaiah 12:2 "Surely God is my salvation; I will trust and not be afraid. The Lord, the Lord is my strength and my song; he has become my salvation."

Mouth:
Isaiah 12:5 "Sing to the Lord, for he has done glorious things; let this be known to all the world."

Hands:
Psalm 47:1: "Clap your hands all you nations."
Feet:
Psalm 30:11 "You turned my wailing into dancing; you removed my sackcloth and clothed me with joy."

In closing, it is time to go EXTREME!! Believers must do the will of God. Although situations come and go, we must be consistent in our praise and worship to our God. God has already worked it out for us. We just have to keep our faith totally reliant upon Him. Never let that falter. God wants to grow you. You just have to go through the process. It is not instantaneous.

Questions for Discussion

Chapter Five
God Has Prepared You For Your Battle

1. Think of some ways God has prepared you for your battle.
2. Based on that, how can you encourage others?

Section One
How Can I Be Strong?

1. Record a personal situation in which God has helped you to be strong.
2. What lesson did God teach you?

Section Two
There's Never Enough Time

1. What are some other ways that you use to be faithful in putting God first?
2. How can you teach others to be faithful in their time with God?

Section Three
Follow The Leader

1. Who has God ordained for you to follow?
2. How can you be a great leader?

Section Four
Trusting God 101

1. What is your trusting God 101 story?
2. Do you still find it hard sometimes to trust God?

Section Five
What's A Father To Do?

1. Do you need God to restore you today? If so, ask Him to.
2. Examine yourself. Are you like the older brother, not ready to reconcile with his younger brother?
3. How can you as a Christian be a participant in the ministry of reconciliation?

Section Six
It Took That

1. What are some personal situations in which you can say, "It took that?"
2. Do you allow your situations to control you or do you allow them to make your praise extreme?
3. Are you allowing God to use your testimony to encourage people? Write about or discuss your experience.

Chapter 6

Opportunity, You've Got It! Do You Want It?

Numbers 13-30-33; 14:26-38

The Israelites teach us a lesson about what to do with opportunity. God brought them to the brink of possession and they decided they didn't want the opportunity. In Numbers, Chapter 13, the Israelites were in an uproar, moved by the doubtful reports of the ten spies. They turned their backs on their opportunity because of fear. They turned their backs on their opportunity because they listened to the voice of man rather than the voice of God. They had spent three hundred years in slavery. They had come across the dessert with challenges of water and challenges of food. They stood at the brink of their opportunity and didn't want it. The men began to cry out an evil report, a report that said they could not meet the challenge. They saw the enemy as a giant and themselves as grasshoppers. It caused the Lord to ask Moses and Aaron why the people were murmuring against Him. God was hearing their complaints. God was hearing the confessions of doubt rather than the confessions of faith. God said in chapter 14, verses 28 through 29 that He would do to them exactly what they said. God said He would honor their confession. He said they would miss the opportunity of the promised land. They would die in the wilderness. Everyone twenty years old or older, who grumbled against God, would not enter the promised land. God said he would pass the opportunity on to their children. It's your opportunity now. You've got it! Do you want it?

Every Life Is Important

"...The kingdom of heaven is like a merchant looking for fine pearls. When he found one of great value, he went away and sold everything he had and bought it." Matthew 13:45-46

Because we live in a day and time when the world measures a man by his outward appearance rather than his inner spirit, so many people feel worthless. Now is a good time for us to make an effort to build one another up. We, as a people, must see who we are and what we can be through Jesus.

In the 13th chapter of Matthew, Jesus shows us how important our souls are to Him. He sets for us an example in knowing the worth of an individual. To God, every soul is a valuable pearl for which He gave all to purchase. He didn't even spare His Son, Jesus. Every person is equally important to God. Jesus died for every one of us; rich and poor, young and old, all people all over the world.

We must let everyone know that they are valuable to God and to the Christian family. Mistakes do not devalue us. The price that Jesus paid covers our mistakes. No one is too common. No one is too unlearned for God to use them. Jesus took a handful of everyday men and made them world-movers. He brought out treasure in them they had never dreamed. It is a lesson we must learn.

It is not what you are, but what you can become in the hands of God. It matters not who you are; but it is who you are and what you are willing to yield to the power of God to become His new creation. The song, "Ordinary People" is so true. God does use ordinary people. He uses people like you and me. Little does become much when you place it in the Master's hands. Don't look at how little you have to offer. Look at your willingness to place yourself in God's hands. If you are willing to place whatever you have and whoever you are in the Master's hands, He will shape and guide your destiny. God's plan is not slowed down because there is a shortage of gifted persons, but rather a shortage of persons who are willing to yield who they are to Him. YOUR LIFE IS IMPORTANT! WILL YOU GIVE IT TO JESUS? Will you give your all to Him?

"The Joy Of Salvation"

Romans 3:24, 4:8, 10:9, John 3:16, 1:12, Romans 6:23

In my reading, I had five questions come to mind. What does it mean to be saved? Well, Romans 3: 24 says, "and *you* are justified freely by his grace through the redemption that came by Christ Jesus." That means that once you're saved, you have been acquitted, and your sins have been detached from you. Romans 4: 8 tells us, "Blessed is the man whose sin the Lord will never count against him."

In other words, you were forgiven by the mercy or compassion of God.

The second question is, how can I be saved? Romans 10:9 says "That if you confess with your mouth, "Jesus is Lord," and believe in your heart that God raised him from the dead, you will be saved. To be saved all you have to do is confess with your mouth and believe in your heart that God raised Jesus from the dead and you will be saved.

The third question is , Is salvation available to everyone? John 3:16 says, "For God so loved the world that he gave his one and only Son, that whoever believes in him shall not perish but have eternal life." This means that anyone can receive salvation by believing in Jesus Christ.

Next, how can I be sure of my salvation? John 1:12 says, "Yet to all who received him, to those who believed in his name, he gave the right to become children of God–"This is saying just as a child can't be unborn, God's children, can't be *unborn* again. In this life, you are born into a family. If you disobey your parents they cannot rescind your birth.

The final question is, why is salvation so central to Christianity? Romans 6:23 says, "For the wages of sin is death, but the gift of God is eternal life in Christ Jesus our Lord. God's free gift to the world is to live forever in His presence. Salvation is key. It is deliverance or liberation from the power of our weaknesses.

As I sign off, I want to leave you with a promise from God. "That if you confess with your mouth, "Jesus is Lord," and believe in your heart that God raised him from the dead, you will be saved." Romans 10:9

The Joy Of Salvation (Part 2)
Three Proofs of Salvation

1 John

I'm going to give you three proofs to help you know that you are saved. These proofs are, *inward, outgoing, and outward*.

1 John 5:1 says, "Everyone who believes that Jesus is the Christ is God's child." (Amplified Bible) This is *inward proof.* You have to truly believe within your heart that Jesus is God's way to save you, and He will deliver you from the sin that has held you captive for so many years. After you have believed and realized that He has rescued you from sin (the desire to disobey God), you will be saved. Jesus releases the Holy Spirit in us and we strive to please God.

1 John 4:7 teaches us about *"outgoing proof"*. "Beloved let us love one another." (Amplified Bible) Love is outgoing, it is what comes from us when we are saved. We love others even when they don't treat us the way we should be treated. Although there are over a hundred scriptures that talk about love, let's examine 1st Corinthians 13: 4-7. It says that love is patient and kind, not jealous or boastful or proud or rude. It doesn't talk about others, nor is it jealous of others. It is God given.

Our actions are *outward proof.* 1 John 2:29 says a true sign that we are God's children is that we strive to do right like Jesus did. Christians have to continually be aware that we are God's example to the world. We are the only way that they can see what God expects because they do not read the Bible.

As I sign off, I want to remind you that Christ has called us to be like Him. We have to believe, love and allow the world to see Christ through us.

A Welcome Shepherd

The Lord is my shepherd; I shall not want." Psalms 23:1

As we grow older , the 23 rd Psalm seems to become more and more meaningful to us when we say, "the Lord is my Shepherd". God is our welcome companion.

Experience has taught us that He is there when no one else is. We are confident that God is watching over us every moment of our lives. We have learned that He sees the dangers we must face long before they reach us. This has taught us to build a great trust in Him. Almost without thinking about it, we whisper a prayer to Him throughout the day saying, 'Lord have mercy', or just, 'Lord help.' God has become so real to us that we trust Him for the big things and small things without ever really thinking about it.

He is our daytime Shepherd, guarding every step that we take. Even though our steps are not as sure and our limbs are not as strong, it makes us constantly aware that it is God who makes us strong. He is our Shepherd, anchoring our hands that are not as steady as they used to be. He leads us along the paths of life for our eyes are not as strong as they once were. We follow Him to the green pastures of food and shelter.

Jesus is our nighttime Shepherd who watches us in the wee hours of the night and keeps us safe. He rocks us to sleep and keeps us company even if we awake in the midnight hour. The comfort we have in knowing that the Lord is truly our Shepherd gives us added confidence as we seek to share our testimony with others. You have within you a treasure. As the generations come behind you, they can hear from you those reassuring words, " I have tried God for myself. The Lord *is* my Shepherd.

How Big Is God?

"Be strong and courageous. Do not be afraid or discourage ... for there is a greater power with us than with him." 2 Chronicles 32: 7

The story is told of a little boy who was frightened of the dark. When the lights were out he began to imagine that all kinds of things were in his room. In trying to console the child, his father told him that God was with him, and he did not have to fear. The little boy thought about what his father said and he thought about his imaginary monster. The little boy asked, "how big is God? This is a pretty big monster."

As we think about this story, it is something we deal with everyday. We wonder if God will measure up to the challenge of our problem. As we face our situations, we deal with them on the basis of whether or not we believe God is big enough to handle them.

Hezekiah, in the above passage of scripture, encourages the people of God to have strength and courage based upon the ability of God. It is sound advice for us today. In this complex world, we face so many situations that are so much bigger than we are. We can know in our hearts that there is no problem, no situation, bigger than our God.

How big is God??? He was bigger than the enemies that would try to capture Israel. Over and over God has proven that He is bigger than famine, bigger than hate, bigger than any monster the enemy would try to paint in our minds.

How big is God??? He is bigger than your greatest need, bigger than your tallest mountain. I've told you how big God is. Now, you tell me, "How Much Do You Trust Him???"

Get Up and Go Down Because God Is Not Through With You

Jeremiah 18:1-5

I want to talk about Jeremiah's journey down to the potter's house. Jeremiah became a prophet by the divine call of God.

"Before I formed you in the womb, I knew and approved of you and before you were born I separated and set you apart, consecrating you; and I appointed you as a prophet to the nations."

(Jeremiah 1:5) God knew you before your mother did, He saw everything that you would do and would go through, and still called you. He called you to a future before you ever had a past. Although you've made mistakes, God still wants you.

In Jeremiah 18, God wants Jeremiah to get up and go down to the potter's house, a place where God can speak to him and show him some things. Where does God want you to get up from? What are you sitting in the midst of that He wants you to get up from and come to a place where there are no distractions? Now you can hear only Him. Just like Jeremiah, you have a call on your life, and that call will lead to the fulfillment of God's promise to you.

As I close, remember that God promised you a future before you ever had a past. Don't let Satan hold the mistakes of your past over you. Focus on your future. Get up and go down to the place where God wants to speak to you. His call leads to your promise. There is a direct connection!

Questions for Discussion

Chapter Six
Opportunity, You've Got It! Do You Want It?

1. What are you doing with the opportunity that God gives you?
2. Is the confession that you've made over your situation one of faith? If not, how will you change it.

Section One
Every Life Is Important

1. How can you allow God to use you to show someone else how valuable they are?
2. How has this lesson changed your sense of self?

Section Two
The Joy Of Salvation

1. Do you have the joy of salvation? If not, get saved today!
2. How has God's free gift transformed you?

Section Three
The Joy Of Salvation (2Part) Three Proofs of Salvation

1. Can you see these outgoing proofs working in your life?
2. Write about or discuss a situation in which these three proofs helped you lead someone to Christ.

Section Four
A Welcome Shepherd

1. Do you remember the first time where you could say that God was truly your shepherd? If so, what happened?
2. Are you sharing your testimonies with future generations?

Section Five
How Big Is God?

1. How much do you trust God?
2. What is your first reaction, faith or fear?

Section Six
Get Up and Go Down Because God Is Not Through With You

1. What things are you asking God to deliver you from so that you can get your promise?
2. Do you know the call of God on your life? If so, what is it?
3. What destiny are you trusting God to take you to?

Chapter 7

Deal Or No Deal (Are You In Or Out?)

Not Too Old For Vision

"...the word of the Lord came to Abram in a vision, Do not be afraid, Abram. I am your shield, your very great reward."
Genesis 15:1

Like most of us, Abraham wanted to know God's plan as it related to his life. He remembered that he had a promise from God, but looked at the age of his body and wondered if it was too late. He began to look around for a back up plan. It's interesting how Sarai, his wife looked at the inability of her body and her substitute was Hagar. Abram looked at his body and his substitute was Eliezer.

Satan will always try to get us to look at alternatives to the vision. But God had made a commitment that did not need a back up plan. There were several components to God's commitment to Abraham. When Abraham was seventy-five years old God promised to make him a great nation, to bless him, make his name great, allow him to be a blessing, to bless those who blessed him, to curse those who cursed him and to bless all the families of the earth through him.

Abraham was not too old for a vision. Abraham believed God and followed as God led. As they walked, they talked. God poured vision into Abraham and Abraham built altars and prayed and worshipped and praised God.

In spite of Abraham's commitment to the vision, things happened in his life that dimmed the vision. There was a famine; his family circle was threatened. His wife tried to give him seed through her servant, Hagar, instead of trusting God for the promise. Lot was kidnapped and Abraham had to go to battle to regain his freedom.

Sometimes the day to day challenges can make you forget the promise of God or weaken your commitment to His plan. And so, God came to Abraham in a vision to remind him not to be afraid, that He would protect and reward him. This time Abraham looked for an alternative. He looked to his servant, Eliezer, to be the channel of blessing. Abraham faced what we face today, man's substitutes or God's provision. To be victorious, we must learn to look beyond what we can see, in order to see the provision of God.

How often has God promised you something and you limited Him to what you could see? God is willing to pour vision into you and bring that vision to pass. Don't let the day to day challenges dim the vision or weaken your commitment to what God has shown. God told Abraham to look up and look into His resources. Start counting the stars (vs. 5). You too must look up and see how limitless God is. When you look at carnal things your vision is blocked, but when you look at spiritual things there are no walls, no barriers. This is a new year and a new opportunity for you. Look up and begin to see what God has already done, and you too will begin to have hope as you live out God's plan for your life.

A Mother's Love

1 Samuel 1:22-28

I want to take a moment to recognize Hannah. Why? Because she loved her son, Samuel, she gave him to God for the rest of his life. Why? Because I have a mother who loves her sons, and she gave us back to God for the rest of our lives, we learned to have a commitment to God.

Hannah was made fun of because she was unable to bear children. It left her in tears and unable to eat. In those days women felt ashamed if they were unable to have children, but more than this, it was the desire of Hannah's heart.

Hannah took her desire to God because she realized that a delay in the fulfillment of the desire of her heart did not mean that it was not going to happen. It just meant that it hadn't happened yet. Hannah prayed. She poured her heart out to God, "Lord ...if you give me a child...I will give him to you all of his life." God answered Hannah's prayer. We learn from Hannah that God is never late, and His delay does not necessarily mean "No," but "Wait."

After Hannah gave birth to Samuel, she did not go back to the temple until she had weaned Samuel. She took the time to build a secure attachment, a stable and positive emotional bond with her son. Each day with his mother was an opportunity to allow Samuel to feel the security of her love.

We see her love for Samuel because she prepared him before she gave him. We see her love for God because she kept her promise and gave back all that God had given her, including her only son. What a tender, yielded heart Hannah had, full of love for her son and full of love for her God.

Whatever you are asking God for, take it to the altar and believe Him to bless you. Just as Hannah did, keep things in perspective. She did not love what she had prayed for more than she loved God. When God blesses you, remember your love and commitment to Him.

Hannah is an example to all mothers to prepare your children and give them to God. Samuel is an example to all children to respond to a mother's love by yielding yourself to God.

I Will Touch The World

"For where two or three come together in my name, there am I with them." Matthew 18:20

Our hearts and spirits can gather in His world in a great prayer meeting. Imagine what will happen as we agree in prayer for God to fulfill His purpose in each life that is yielded to Him. We have the promise of God that He will be among us.

Make a commitment to touch the world with your prayer life. Reach out to God on behalf of others. Pray beyond your needs and the needs of your family. There is no greater need in our world than the impact of a praying people. Turn every complaint into a prayer. Pray for those who are unfair to you and do not understand your needs. Pray for those who suffer hunger and poverty. Together we can touch the world!

Prayer seems so small in the scheme of things that move the world. Often, when our backs are against the wall we say, "All I can do is pray." We say it as though we are somehow limited in power, as though it is our last resort after trying everything else. Yet, we have learned from science that most often the smaller and less visible something is, the more powerful it is. Louis Pasteur showed us that bacteria ten times smaller than a flea can kill a man. Physicists say that a cosmic ray is more penetrating and more potent than a ray of the sun. And of course, we've all used the expression, "TNT comes in small packages."

You are one person on planet earth, but God has placed you here to touch the world. Most of us would not like to think of having lived our lives without contribution. There is something within us that wants to give back to life. Most people dare to think of having an impact on another life, but fear moving outside of our comfort zones. We can reach beyond what we have allowed to become our small world and tread a path that leads to serving others. All it takes is a servant heart. Everyone can serve others. Some can serve by spending their time, while others can serve by financing those who feel called to full time ministry.

Ministry needs those who can spend hours in prayer and counseling. Just as one person may have the gift to write or teach, there are those God has called to pray in the trenches of life. Offering more than words through an inner commitment to bridging the gap between need and resource, prayer warriors are used by God to break the grip of the enemy daily.

Prayer is reverence for God, a trust in His ability to effect the situations we face. Our thoughts and words describe conditions. Our faith shows that we trust God to change those conditions. Prayer takes time and commitment to engage in conversation with God about the need for His involvement in our circumstances. Prayer and faith work together. They are an investment in kingdom building. Intercessory prayer is based upon a relationship with God and those we petition for. It is caring enough to pray. Sometimes we think we have to be saying or doing something to make an impact on our world, but what you pray speaks much louder than what you say.

"Never Give Up"

1 John 2: 14

I want to look at quitting. How does God feel about quitting? Well, He gave Paul a letter to give to the Galatians saying*"... We must not give up*

How do we "keep from giving up"? Avoid discouragement by focusing on Him and His word. Psalm 29:11 says " The Lord will give strength to His people that will not fold under pressure. He will give strength that no enemy can penetrate." God has given you strength that can not be broken. 1 John 2: 14 says, "… because you are strong and vigorous…"

God has called you "strong," so no matter what anybody says, whether it's your family or people who say that they're your friends, don't forget that God called you "strong." Vigorous is physical or mental strength. Strength is dunamis in its original Greek, meaning power. So God has given you the power or the ability to be victorious over the devil, not only physically, but mentally as well. So, you can't allow the enemy to have free reign over your mind because God gave you the power to defeat him.

As I close, know that you are strong, both physically and mentally. God has already strengthened you. He has already given you everything you need, so avoid discouragement and keep yourself strengthened by reading the word of God and praying every day. God bless you!

God Wants You!!!

"Notice among yourselves, dear brothers, that few of you who follow Christ have big names or power or wealth...God has chosen to use ideas the world considers foolish..." 1 Corinthians 1:26,27

There is so much God wants us to do. Why not ask Him what He would have you do? Many times we want to do what God would have us do, but we question our ability. Consider these things:

- The more reasons you can list why God shouldn't use you, the more He sees you as a prime candidate for service (2 Corinthians 4:7). God does not call anyone to service that He does not qualify (Jeremiah 1:1-10).
- The more you look at yourself and see what disqualifies you for service, the more God wants to use you. When He uses you for service, others will know that it is the power of God through you, and they will glorify Him (1 Corinthians 1:26-30).
- Do you look at your life and see weakness? Do you feel rejected and worthless? Do you feel too old, too young, or too unprepared? God wants you. In fact, you're the very person He wants to enlist! Through you, Jesus can shine. Look at the apostle Paul's experience (2 Corinthians 12:9-10). A good Christian leader does not rely on his own strength but looks to God from which comes his strength.
- God will take any painful experience you've had and use your healing for His glory. You must take who you are and what you have experienced, both good and bad, and offer it to Him. Make an exchange, His healing for your pain. If you will yield every talent, every ability, every weakness and every strength to the Lord, He will use those things to bear fruit for Himself.

Stir up the gift of God in you!

You Have Been Sent!

"When Jesus had called the twelve together he gave them power and authority to drive out all demons and to cure diseases, and he sent them out to preach the kingdom of God and to heal the sick."
Luke 9:1,2

My challenge to you is to operate under the covering which Christ has sent you. That covering is power and authority. Power and authority are necessary to do what Christ has given you to do as you go where He sends you. If Jesus had said take your shoes, you know how to pick up your shoes and put them on. That request is easily understood. If He had said take a lunch, most of you can pack a lunch. You can see shoes. You can touch a lunch, but how do you take power and authority with you?

Jesus gives you the same weapons He gave His disciples, " power and authority." Where do you get it and how do you use it? These questions have caused many to stumble. Sometimes power and authority are confused. Power has to do with the ability to do something. Authority is to have God's permission to use His power in a given situation because He has put control in your hands. As an example, consider your vehicle. There is gas in it, and it is in working order so there is power to drive it at an intersection no matter what color the light is. You, however, know that green, yellow and red lights have been placed there for your safety. Green gives you the authority to go, red to stop, and yellow to operate with caution. Just as you operate your empowered vehicle according to the authority given by the color of a light signal, you must use the power God has given with His permission. Authority means God has put you in charge. As God passes on His permission to you, use the power He has given to change lives and situations.

Faith is the key that unlocks power and authority. Satan uses the absence of immediate results to discourage many people from using the gifts that God has given. Some miss the gift because they overlook the step of mastering these tools. Christ says , "my peace I leave with you." So, the peace is here! Christ has left it, but you must master it's use. As you use what God gives you, understand that you become more skilled. As you become more skilled, your faith increases. Power and authority are tools, but the use of these tools must be mastered.

You read about power and authority in others like Paul, but you are not privy to their step by step growth. When your mastery is not instant, you sometimes lose courage. In Luke 19:11-27, Jesus gives us a very good example of power and authority in the parable of the nobleman and the ten servants. The nobleman represents Christ, and you and I represent those servants. To ten servants Jesus gave ten pounds and authority by saying, "Occupy til I come".

Just as Jesus stood apart from the old way, they too would stand out in a crowd. The difference was, both the old and the new way carried teaching, carried a sermon, carried a message, but with the new way came a miracle that followed the sermon because of the gift of authority. Their question was, Mark 1:27 *"What is this? A new teaching! With authority he commands even the unclean spirits, and they obey him."* The Greek word is "sunzeteo" which means they started to seek and examine what was going on. For them this was a (Greek) "kainos", which meant new. This was something they had heard of but the teaching now had power. This was a new "didache", which meant doctrine or teaching. These disciples got excited. Jesus could speak something and make it happen. You have been sent into homes, into churches, into hospitals. God has a word for you to give and He wants it given with power and authority. Words are just words unless power lifts them into the receptive part of the heart of man. Words are just words unless they raise up a standard of authority against the destruction of the enemy.

Authority and power are gifts. Jesus called the twelve together and gave them power and authority. Even Judas, though he did not use it, had power and authority over the enemy. Judas could have put the enemy to flight rather than yielding to the enemy. You stand in position to have the power of the resurrected Christ come through you because you have been sent. An officer of the law has both right and responsibility because he or she stands behind a badge. You have both right and responsibility because you stand behind the authority of the resurrected Christ working through you.

To execute power and authority, faith must see faith. Jesus had faith, but before He executed deliverance in the lives of others, He identified and called forth their faith. The faith in Him acted upon the faith in them. When the four friends dug through the roof so that the paralyzed man could be healed (Luke 5:20), Jesus didn't look at the commitment they had to their friend, or the physical strength they had between them to carry the man. Nor did He look at the determination they had to dig a hole in the roof when there was no possibility to enter through the door. Scripture says, "...and when Jesus saw *their faith*, he said to the paralytic, "my son, your sins are forgiven." (Mark 2:5) Faith had to see faith. Time and time again you witness faith seeing faith. Two blind men were following Jesus crying out for mercy (Matthew 9:27-34). Jesus asked if they believed He could do it. They confessed their faith. Faith had to see faith. Jesus touched their eyes and said, "according to your faith it will be done." In other words, the power of the pounds is in your hands until I return from receiving my kingdom. Even though some did not like it and asked the nobleman to hurry and return home, the nobleman's expectation was that they take charge and multiply what he had put in their hands. Christ has put something in your hands and He expects you to reign over it; have authority over it until He returns.

Power of authority was new to those Jesus spoke to. Jesus was teaching his followers about the delegation of authority. The word used for authority means "out of". Jesus was teaching the disciples that He would act out of Himself to give them the power of authority. They had witnessed the authority of Christ. He was now teaching them that He would work that authority through them, and that this would empower their ministry. They would have his permission to use the authority that came through Him.

To execute power and authority you must also pray. The sermon has ended. The miracle has happened. While others slept , Jesus went aside to pray (Mark 1:35). Scripture says Jesus went out into a lonely place. It was He and the Father in conversation. It was an opportunity to bathe his soul, rest, and be replenished in privacy with His Father. Here He could pour out the challenges of the day and be refilled with new hope, new strength, and new power from the Father. What an example for you to follow! It is not good to place one day's challenges on top of another, but rather, you should have your time with God to release and be refilled.

My wife, the daughter of a pastor, shares how she had witnessed her parents giving of themselves to members of the congregation. They never said they were too tired, but somehow mustered the energy to respond whenever they were called upon. As a result, she gave and gave of herself, and only went to God for refilling when she was near spiritual exhaustion. She washed dishes, cooked dinner, helped the boys with their homework and ministered on the telephone at the same time. So to pull away from everything seemed an impossibility. She didn't know how. When she went to seminary, Dr. Anne Wimberly taught her the importance of refilling. It is an art to be learned. The class exercises she received that took her through the process frustrated her. She constantly said she didn't have time for the assignment. She had other important things to do. God led me to tell her to schedule an appointment with Him, and just sit for two hours and not to let anything interrupt the appointment. Although she could not imagine just sitting for two hours, she agreed to try it. I took care of our sons as she spent the two hours with God. What a rewarding lesson! Thereafter, this has become such an important part of her ministry. To execute power and authority in its fullness, there must be time to pull away from everything and everybody to pour out and to be poured into.

To execute power and authority, the person being delivered must be willing to be made clean. One thing that discourages a person sent by God is when the one who needs healing or growth does not want it. They may ask for it, but they may not be willing to do what it takes to get it. You will read in scripture the example given by Jesus. A young man (Mark 10:17) ran up to Jesus and fell on his knees. He asked how he could inherit eternal life, but when Jesus told him what he needed to do, he walked away.

Picture this in your mind's eye. Blind Bartimaeus is calling out to Jesus (Mark 10:47) for mercy. Jesus can see that he is blind, yet He asked, "What do you want me to do for you?" In Mark 1:40, the leper was willing to turn loose the leprosy and cling to Jesus. He was willing to be cleansed of what had held him bound. The young man was unwilling to sell out. For this ruler, the price was too high to obtain eternal life. On the other hand, Bartimaeus wanted to see, he was willing to be healed. The person being delivered must want to be made clean.

Know this. God has given you both power and authority. Perhaps you did not reach the heights to which you aspired last year, or maybe you have fallen. You can get back up again. Have the godly confidence of your call and the willingness to receive his gift of empowered authority. God has put you in charge. You have the power and authority, God's gift of ability and His permission to be in command. It's God's battle, but your victory!

Questions for Discussion

Chapter Seven
Deal or no Deal (Are You In Or Out?)

Section One
I Will Touch The World

1. How can God use you to touch the world?
2. What are you doing daily to make sure that you are offering yourself up willingly to God as His vessel?

Section Two
A Mother's Love

1. What is the desire of your heart that is yet unfulfilled?
2. Once you receive that desire, will you dedicate it to be used for the glory of God?

Section Three
Never Give Up

1. Do you trust God enough to know that He will bring His word to pass in your life?
2. What do you do when you feel like quitting?

Section Four
Not Too Old For Vision

1. What vision has God given you?
2. What alternatives are you using?

Section Five
God Wants You!

1. What are some things that make you think that God can't use you?

2. How is God changing your mindset based on this teaching?

Section Six
You've Been Sent

1. In what ways have you been loosed to operate in the power and authority that God has given you?
2. Are you willing to be made clean?

Printed in the United States
73948LV00004B/325-453